MW01115998

WHAT THEY DIDN'T
TEACH YOU IN

FANCY
LEADERSHIP
SCHOOL

A Guide For
SUCCESSFUL SCHOOL
LEADERSHIP

DR. MARK WILSON

What They Didn't Teach You in Fancy Leadership School

ISBN: 979-8-9884571-0-7

Cover design by Mark Wilson using a Canva Template

Certain images used in this book have been sourced from Canva, a graphic design platform. These images are used consistent to the licensing rules as set by Canva at https://www.canva.com/help/licenses-copyright-legal-commercial-use/

Published by Principal Matters! Publishing

308 Merriman Trail
Anderson, SC 29621
United States of America

mark.wilson.ga@gmail.com
principal-matters.com

Printed in Anderson, SC, USA by Attaway Printers
First Printing, 2023

Dedicated to

ALL of the leaders of school systems who have
entrusted me to coach their school leaders over the past dozen
years. Thank you.

ALL of the principals, assistant principals, and aspiring leaders
who have made it a joy to serve them as their "principal teacher,"
THANK YOU for the privilege to be a part of your leadership
journey.

This book represents the things I've learned from you. It's my
pleasure to share insights from your journeys with other leaders
everywhere.

TABLE OF CONTENTS

INTRODUCTION

The expert at anything was once a beginner.

~Helen Hayes

First off, I really like *Fancy Leadership Schools* and my friends who work at them. The name of this book isn't meant to be derisive in any way. It comes from one of the brand new principals I had the privilege to work with.

After having completed the session and her first few years as a principal, Dr. Liz Raeburn told a newly-hired principal that he should take one of my workshops. She said, "Dr. Wilson will teach you *what they didn't teach you in fancy leadership school.*"

I'd had other titles picked out for this book, but after hearing that... well, it's catchy even if it's not completely true. For one, they DO teach you a lot of very important things in traditional educator leadership programs. Having spent time with colleagues in higher education, I know the valuable work they do to prepare school leaders, and that many of their topics are the same as those you see here. I think a lot of these topics do get covered in "fancy leadership school," so nothing but love from me for all of my higher ed friends.

Meanwhile, here's my story: *I was a teacher and a coach, and then a principal. Now, I teach and coach principals.* Since 2012, I've been in full-time support of school leaders with a clear focus to help them lead schools. The work I do is job-embedded, highly-practical, and personalized for those with whom I'm privileged to serve.

When I left the principal's office to begin this chapter of my career, my first move was to travel across North America and speak at conferences from near to far. Like you, I'd spent most of my life in a schoolhouse, so I was amazed and excited to get out... see new things. The people I met everywhere? Great. We are a part of a brotherhood and sisterhood of caring and compassionate people who want to do good for others.  That's what I found wherever I would go. My time on the circuit was rewarding financially, a joy to do, and took me to new places with wonderful people. There was, however, something missing for me. After all of those years as teacher, coach, and administrator, it turns out that I had grown fond of being around not just for the kickoff, but for the whole game. Sure, I enjoy speaking to a crowd, encouraging them, and getting them enthused about the work they're doing. The people who do that for us in education play an important role to "pour into" teachers and administrators everywhere.

That's when I made a shift and began to focus on a slightly smaller "classroom," ... my home state of Georgia. My work was supported by the Georgia Department of Education, the Georgia Professional Standards Commission, through Georgia's Sixteen RESAs (Regional Educational Service Agencies), as well as the company *Thinking Maps*. The kind people in each of those organizations afforded me the opportunity, on different occasions, to reach out to new principals across Georgia. In over a decade of this work, I've delivered hundreds and hundreds of workshops, classes, and conferences to thousands of school leaders. While

I've specifically worked to support our new and newer principals, I've also worked with assistant principals and aspiring leaders as well as central office leaders and Boards of Education.

I was a school administrator for fifteen years, but this isn't a memoir or me pontificating about my time in the principal's chair. Leadership coaching has given me insight I didn't have when I was the principal. Then, I only had a few school administrators I had seen up close; now, I have hundreds.

The purpose of this book is pretty simple; I have the privilege to be in different schools most every week. I'm able to be behind the scenes with principals like a National Geographic documentary. I want to share those experiences with you, via this book. The things I've learned from 7,500 school visits and counting, condensed into these sections and pages, in the hopes that it will help you in your work.

These experiences have taught me a lot about new principals:
- *What makes them struggle;* (pride, ineffective working relationship with assistant principal(s), poor communication)
- *What makes them soar;* (confidence, making connections and building relationships, humility)
- *What is most likely to reach up from the turf and tackle them mid-run.* (things that didn't have anything to do with them, failure to listen, trying to go too far too fast)

This is your book now and you can read it in whatever manner you choose, but here's how it's put together. There are 71 chapters that are all intentionally short so you can read a little at a time if you choose to do so. The chapters go together in nine thematic sections if you like to chunk your learning. Finally, the whole book *is* connected if you are a binge-watcher. Whatever works for you.

Here we go!

Part I. Kickoff

READ THIS FIRST

The New Principal:
Guiding Principles for Success

Priority *Your ultimate goal as a first-year principal is to become...* *a second-year principal.*	Smile. Enjoy the Journey.	*Begin thinking of your legacy at the beginning, not the end.* *What others join you in imagining, creating, and implementing will last longer than things you do by yourself.*
You got the job by being smart, talented, committed, and capable. You'll keep the job by leading others to be smart, talented, committed, and capable.	Your most critical school relationship? The one with your AP. Invest time in it.	Visit Classrooms Every Day No excuses.
Be an effective listener.	Earning the position gets you in the door. To be the leader, people have to give you their permission to lead them.	*By Halloween, the faculty and staff will have made their minds up as to whether you are a trick or a treat. First impressions are often lasting ones.*
Perfection is the enemy of progress. It keeps you from trying the things that may make the most difference.	Sleep. 7 Hours/Night. *Take care of yourself. You have what you need for success, but you need to be at your best to do your best.*	Having a good idea is just the beginning. Implementing those ideas well, however, is the measure of effective leadership.

In case you have recently been named principal (like last week or something) and have *very* little time to read, the chart on the previous page is there especially for you. The twelve nuggets on the graph are there sort of like a first-aid kit. If you don't have time right now for more, please ponder those items.

Based on all of the practical interactions I've had with school administrators, those are twelve that I know you need as you start.

BE YOURSELF

To be yourself in a world that is constantly trying to make you something else is the greatest accomplishment.

~Ralph Waldo Emerson

In my work with new and newer principals, I've seen many enthusiastic and well-meaning leaders expend a lot of time and energy trying to figure out who to be. Who is it that the superintendent wants me to be? Who do the teachers want me to be? Did they like the last principal and should I be like her? Did they not like the last principal and I need to be the opposite? Nearly everyone goes through a process of trying to determine how they are going to interact with the people of the school. It always comes back to this: be yourself.

If you try being anyone other than yourself, it will be like you're wearing someone else's shoes ...on the wrong feet … in the shower. While this may seem to be the simplest piece of advice you've ever heard, it's a lot more difficult than you think. When you're the principal, all eyes are on you. You get a lot of questions, a ton of requests, and buckets of problems people bring you to solve.

You speak in front of large groups; you meet individually with parents; you join a grade level for professional learning. You're everywhere, in the middle of everything, around everybody. You want to do a good job; you want to be a good leader; you want to serve your people and your school.

Here's the problem: the people around you don't all come together on a definition of *what* you do as the principal, even less, *how* you do it. You are not the first principal they have ever seen, so they have established a frame of reference from which they can't be shaken. Everyone around you… students, teachers, parents, central office… has a vision of what they think 'principal' is, what they do, and how they do it. And… they don't all have the same idea of what that looks like! And… they don't always (well, they actually rarely) communicate what the picture of 'principal' is running through their head. It's most likely been formed by their experience, maybe good experience, maybe bad. What they are hoping/expecting/counting on you to be, to do, and to say is shaped by the ghosts of principals past… who you may or may not have met.

If you spend your time trying to guess what they want you to do, how they want you to act, *who they want you to be*, you'll expend a lot of energy and invest a lot of time, only to find out that you can't be everything to everybody. (Note: This is not an invitation to forego empathy or be indifferent to your people… please read the book in its entirety. Thank you.)

You need to know yourself, and to be yourself. They hired you. The unique and wonderful you. Be you--- be an ever-improving and always-learning version of you -- but be you. (A good reason never to present yourself as something you're not in an interview.)

By The Way…Don't Try to Please Everybody

You literally can't make everybody happy. *(It's not a great strategy to make everybody mad, either.)* There are conflicting agendas among your constituents, so if you are seeking universal wish-granting to build a peaceable kingdom, well, good luck. What is a more successful strategy is to, over time, help your people unite into a collective vision of success for your school and the people who are in it. To think beyond their own interests… to exchange comfort for good. This takes time. Lots of time. While you're on the way to that level, don't burn out all of your energy on lower-level pursuits.

Example: the teachers who have homerooms have more administrative duties regarding grading and paperwork than the activity teachers. Those homeroom teachers come to you to ask that the activity teachers cover morning *and* afternoon duties to help lighten their load. A new principal might see that as a 'win' and say yes to the plan… but in the process making one group happy at another's expense.

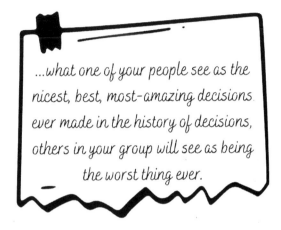

…*what one of your people see as the nicest, best, most-amazing decisions ever made in the history of decisions, others in your group will see as being the worst thing ever.*

A wiser approach is to listen, to learn, and to see the implications of your decisions before you react. If you've made it to the position of principal, you've been around school for a while and you are able to see patterns of how things relate to each other. What you might do is to bring both groups together to work on the plan for the following year? There are many possible responses, but this much is true: you have a unique role in the school ecosystem as the sole person who is looking out for *everyone's* interests, not just some. That's why it's hard to please everyone-- they don't have the perspective that you have as the leader, the one that's looking out for everyone.

DO YOUR JOB

If employees feel you don't trust them to do their jobs correctly and well, they'll be reluctant to do much without your approval. On the other hand, when they feel trusted, that you believe they'll do the right things well, they'll naturally want to do things well and be deserving of your trust.

~Mac Anderson

I have coached hundreds of new leaders. As they begin their work in a new job, here are a few of the things they most frequently pop up during the first months:

1. I can't get it all done;
2. I need help managing my time;
3. I'm working all the time.

When you begin a new job, it makes sense you wouldn't be as good at it from the beginning as you were years after doing your old job? Let's focus on the position of principal, although this is transferable to most any job.

If you become the principal, chances are you were good at being a teacher. Then you became an instructional coach, or maybe went straight to assistant principal. You figured that job out and now… the big time! You're the principal of the school. Be reasonable with yourself… you worked hard for a long time to become effective as an AP… you *shouldn't* think you are going to be as good on day one as principal as you were on day 801 as AP!

What can slow your growth in your new job is *failing to make the shift to your new job.* When you *don't know* how to do your new job, it's easy to find yourself doing the things that you *do* know how to do. You know, some of the AP's work.

Much of the work of the assistant principal is task-driven. The majority of the work of the principal is people-driven. It's more about you *and other people* than you may have experienced as assistant principal. It's a lot easier to get rid of wasps on the playground than to reinvigorate a teacher who has lost her zeal for teaching.

So, back to those issues above... getting things done, managing time, working long days. As the principal the pathway to your success begins with *figuring out what your job really is.* Here's a practical way to begin that... begin each day with your journal and jot down a goal or two (no more than three!) for the day. Those goals will look different than your old job (if you're doing it right). For example, your goal as  AP may have been to develop the remediation rotations for third grade; your goal as principal? *Help Mrs. Jones be effective in her job.*

Start the day in your journal with what you hope to accomplish that day. End it with the answer to this question: *who did I help get better at their job today?*

The secret to your job as principal is to *help other people get better at theirs.* With time and focus, you'll find that you are able to get more done in less time when you **begin** with helping others do their job. If you spend your time doing others' jobs, you'll forever have the sensation that you can't get it done.

Leadership is simple. It's not easy. It begins with you understanding you, and goes next to you understanding the nature of your job. From there you can build a team that can accomplish great things together.

Reflect on you work regularly.

In classes, I've often done an exercise called "what's your job?" It goes like this... people work in pairs and ask each other (one at a time) a set of twenty questions. They can ask whatever they choose for the odd numbered questions (why did you get into education? What's your favorite hobby?) but for ALL of the even numbered questions, you simply ask, "what's your job?"

So, in rapid fire succession, you answer questions about school, your life, your work and in between each one you are faced with the question of what is your job. The results are exciting to watch. Almost always, someone's answer about their job changes from the beginning to the end.

If you want to be better in your job, continue to explore *what specifically you are doing that makes the school and its people effective.* A good practice would be to pick a day each month for "What's My Job?" day in your journal. What great insight you'll find when you look back to see how your idea of what your job is changes over time! It is also a GREAT item to bring up intentionally and regularly with your administrative team. Want your APs to perform better? Ask them every month what their job is. If they get a handle on that, you'll be able to get to your job more regularly.

BE VISIBLE

As a leader, part of the job is to be visible and willing to communicate with everyone.

~Bill Walsh

If you're a new principal, chances are you've heard this advice from lots of people already. Be visible. Who's going to argue with that? I mean, what's the alternative, being invisible? So, YES, everyone sets off into their principalship knowing that this nugget is golden and they're definitely going to do it.

But. Not everyone actually does.

Look, it's really hard, because there are so many people you are trying to please. You want the superintendent to be happy with your work; you need to form a team with your faculty and staff; you want to listen to your students and partner with their parents. There are meetings… SO MANY meetings, and there are people who want to see you, and you need to do observations, and then there's a discipline issue that rises to your level. It's really hard to know what to do and what to let others do. It's difficult to balance all of the demands on you in this job. But, being visible IS how you get your job done.

You are the walking, talking, high-fiving, smiling, giver of opportunities, symbol of your school. You're like Mickey Mouse at Disney World; you're in the middle of all of the pictures. It's a role that you play. Maybe you love the limelight, maybe you don't, but being the "mayor" of your school is one of the roles you've been cast for.

It's deeper than that though. If vision, expectations and focus are your job (which we argued earlier in this book), then you have to be *out there* to communicate (another part of your job) those things. If you are sporadic in your presence, you'll seem like a visitor in a place that ought to be your home. But, if you're there, in the classrooms, in the hallways, talking to teachers on their planning periods, speaking to kiddos at lunch, connecting with bus drivers, sitting down with the cafeteria staff, learning everybody's names… well, then people begin to see you as something more than a visitor. They begin to see you as a symbol of consistency. Something (actually someone) they can count on being at that part of the hall every day when they are on the way to third period. The friendly face in the middle of the atrium that speaks to them every day. The person who checks in on you because they know you have been having a hard time with this class.

You bring a sense of safety, security, and presence to the people in your building. They give you their permission to be their leader *after* they begin to trust you, and they begin to trust you when they see you. Consistently. Saying hello. Asking them what they're excited about. Listening.

Do you *really* think that being visible matters? If you do, you'll get out there. Between classes. To start the day. When the teachers are coming in the building. You want to be where the people are. (Shoutout to Ariel) That's where you become their leader.

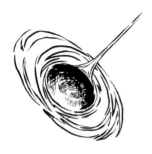

According to NASA at their website, _A black hole is a place in space where gravity pulls so much that even light can not get out._

Just like your office. Stay away. It's no place for you to be. Its force is so great you will never be able to get out and you'll be stuck in there forever.

Do you ever take things to Goodwill? You know, gather things together that you would like to rid yourself of? Then you drive them to your local drop-off center and leave them there. That moment when you leave the drop off center a smile comes over your face. Pure bliss.

That's how many teachers and others feel when they come to your office. They gather up the things that they don't want to hold any more: problems, questions, struggles with other people. They bring them to your office where you sit on high awaiting for such deliveries. They leave them there and turn away with the same joy that you do as you drive away from Goodwill. And they enjoy it so much that the first thing they do when they get back to their room is think about what else they can bring to you!

Don't fall into that mental model of what the principal does. Get out of your office and be among your people. It is their trust you need to earn and their actions you need to influence for you to lead the school in the way you want to lead them. You're not gonna change the world from your office or through an email. If you could, you could just wear pajamas every day. It's not that simple though. No matter what your vision for the school is, no matter what values you all have coalesced around, that vision and those values are in a constant state of definition. You have to be out there, with your people, to be able to embed your instruction and vision and values to them.

You will need to make sure that your people know what you're doing, especially if your predecessor was an office-dweller. It's pretty easy, actually. I asked my faculty to contact Mrs. Segrest (the World's-Greatest Executive Assistant) if they needed to see me. If they needed me right away, she'd get me there. If they needed me sometime that day, she'd make sure that happened too. If they needed to let me know something or get information to me, *they sent the email to her* and she and I would work on it when we met.

It was much more efficient. No lines of teachers wasting their precious time waiting to see me during their planning period. And, when you're out in the building, you can more efficiently and effectively communicate as needed because you're out there and people can conduct business with you then and there.

What about the paperwork I have to do?

Well, get a nice bookbag. Pack some post-it notes, some snacks, your computer, and duck into a classroom while you're out in the building. Let the teacher know you need to answer some emails so you'll be hanging out but you're just getting work done.

(Note: This is a good thing to do with newer teachers. You get to spend time with them and help them not be nervous about you being there, and if the students have been less-than-ideal in their behavior, they'll be sure to put their best foot forward while you're there.) Win-win-win. And, you get some paperwork done while you're in the people-work world. They won't track you down when you're "observing a classroom" so get out there.

You're the principal of the school, not the office manager, so train your office staff and then spend your time with students and teachers.

Visibility doesn't end at dismissal.

There will be much said in this book about finding a balance between work and life. About the need to not work all the time… to not think about work every waking minute. That's all true and important. So is being visible at school events. *Especially* at the beginning of your tenure.

Like it or not, the many people who are watching you from the beginning are going to decide which narrative about you they will buy into. With the exceptions of the occurrence of BIG things and/or a sequence of gaffes or big successes, *people hang onto their original appraisal of you* and it becomes their basis for how they see you and how they approach you. For example, if you stay in the office and get all of the paperwork done, sometimes shutting the door… days without seeing all of your teachers, your teachers *may* begin to think you're not reachable or approachable. And, just like the "telephone game" the story about you gets a little more added to it at each telling.

Choose the narrative. When you first become principal, go to all the things. (Arrive late– leave early) People feel valued when you give them your single greatest gift…your presence. Showing up is half of the deal.

All grade bands are equally important. They don't have an equal number of afternoon and evening activities though. Whatever grade band you're working in, establish yourself at the very start as the principal who shows up. THAT visibility is the best thing you can do for yourself. When the parent sees you at the games…paying attention to the game… being a supporter of your teacher and a cheerleader for your students… they are more likely to give you some grace if and when you are in need of it. If you do these things VERY frequently at the early days of your principalship, the story about you will be that you show up. As time goes by, you don't have to *quite* show up as often to still be known as such. If you miss it at the beginning, you'll be going to everything for years in an attempt to change the primacy bias about you as a visible leader.

I've shared the strategic reasons a principal needs to present during the school day and at after-school events. Please don't hear that as a suggestion that being there to support your folks is a means to an end. This may sound like a lot, but, *if you don't really want to be there, people are going to notice that too.* Yes… arrive after it starts and leave before it ends… but in between **be present in the moment.** And that moment is about cheering for the school of which you are the leader.

It truly helps to genuinely enjoy going to chorus concerts, art shows, and sporting events and everything else. Get your heart right and view them as a privilege to attend. Get to know your students through their lives outside of the classroom and they'll bring a little extra to their work in it. Take freeze pops to band camp on a hot day. Have a special thing with each of your teams and organizations. Figure out the schedule for this in advance and spread it out. You are a big deal to the citizens of your school. Be grateful for that and embed yourself into the happenings there during school and beyond.

In your attempt to be visible and spread love and joy from the principal's office *don't forget people.* Despite that passage that says love doesn't keep score, school people often do.

In other words, spread the love around. Yep, that means you wake up early on Saturday morning to drive two hours each way to see your ROTC drill team perform for about ten minutes. Remember– *this is just as important to these kids and their parents as the football game the night before was to those folks.*

Now there's too many events to make it to everything, but if significant trophies (state or regional champs, for example) are on the line, that's a good time to go. If you make sure you go to at least one event from all of your folks, most everyone will appreciate your effort and your genuine care for their team, their kids, and them. So, get your spreadsheet ready, keep up with it (with your assistant's help) and enjoy the opportunity to be such a big honking deal. It won't last forever.

DEVELOP RELATIONSHIPS

Relationships are everything and great leaders are masters at relationship building.

~Diana Osagie

You've worked hard, earned advanced degrees, distinguished yourself as a teacher and as an assistant principal, and now you have earned the position of *principal*. Congratulations, and a job well done. You truly should be proud of yourself for what you've accomplished.

Now. It's time to lead.

The Board of Education has offered you the position of principal. What they *can't* guarantee is that anyone will listen to you, follow your lead, or join you in the journey you'll be leading. That part is up to you. They give you a position, but now it's up to you to get *permission* to lead.

What you gain from that permission is access to the most important tool you'll use as a principal... influence.

It works like this. You've been put into a position and *now* that you're there the people in charge want you to improve performance. The challenge... there's not an express lane to high performance. It follows a series of deliberate efforts, illustrated here:

HOW TO IMPROVE PERFORMANCE

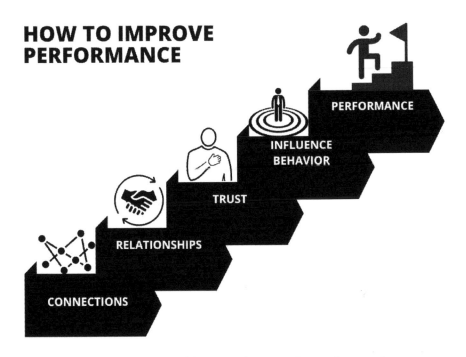

Leaders can be tempted to skip steps in an order to fast track performance. The path looks different to do that… more like force + compliance. It's arduous, climate killing, and not sustainable.

It's why many new principals struggle. They've been placed into a situation in which the timeline for performance doesn't align with the process for success. Only about half of principals are in the same school beyond year three.

That sort of turnover stunts the growth of our schools and keeps this carousel spinning. The more frequently that leadership changes, the more challenging it is for *new* leadership to get permission from the faculty and staff to lead. To get to the place of **trust.**

That's when you've been given permission to be the leader. When they trust you, at least to the degree that you're able to work together and deepen the bonds of trust through joint experience and some level of success.

I was speaking at a national conference a few years ago, and a bright-eyed, enthusiastic leader met me afterwards and asked if we could talk for a little bit. He told me that he had just been named the principal of a large high school the week before. I congratulated him and told him what an honor it is to lead a school. Then he asked this: *They've told me that I have one year to turn the school around. What advice do you have?* I asked him if he was a drinking man… because if he was he should have a drink, and if he wasn't, was he willing to start.

Make progress in a year? Absolutely. Turn the whole thing around in a year…not likely, because you can't place an arbitrary time schedule on trust. And without trust, you don't *really* have permission to lead. And without permission to lead, your influence is limited. Then, you get forced behavior (what people *have* to do to keep their job) instead of chosen behavior (what people do because they've decided to do so).

If you're a new principal, you need to understand this as you begin: they don't know you as their principal yet, so they can only trust you so much.. Even if you were a teacher there, and then you were an assistant principal, you haven't been their principal before and they have to get to know you in *that* role. Don't let it hurt your feelings. It's not personal. (Very little of it ever is.) It's part of the continuum. Teachers (and students and their parents as well) have to trust you if they're going to join you in a journey of success. They need time to see what you're about. To get to know you (or to get to know you in this role). To see how you treat people, to see if you know what you're doing.

Before the clay hardens…

You've got about ninety days for the people around you to develop a solid opinion of you as the leader. In other words, you've got

until Halloween for them to decide whether you're a trick or a treat. Before that, the clay is still hardening. The jury is still out. Somewhere around November 1, they are able to authoritatively have an opinion on the question, *how's the new principal?*

So, be yourself, and be confident. Make connections with others.

There was a new principal I was coaching a few years ago. I went to visit on the Friday before Labor Day, and as we walked together around the school, I asked what he was proud of so far. He said, "I know about half of everybody's names," to which I replied, "hey, that's pretty good to know that many students by now since you've only seen them for a month or so."

He said, "I'm not talking about the students. I'm talking about the teachers."

I stopped in my tracks. *You only know half of the teachers' names?*

He said, "I'm not really good with names, but I'm getting there!"

My role as a coach, I've always believed, is more of an anthropologist. I'm there to observe, but not to direct. At that moment, however, I dropped that role and asked, "do you have a

yearbook class?" They were meeting at that time. I asked the principal to get someone from
the class to come to his office. When they arrived, we asked that they go and get a photo of each faculty and staff member in the school. To please tell them it's a yearbook project. And, to print the pictures, write the names on each one, and return them to the principal as soon as possible. The pair of students enthusiastically set out on their work and I offered this to my new principal.

You have an extra day this weekend. Please go home and learn everyone's name. If you don't know everyone's name by Tuesday, take a personal day and stay home until you know them all. He laughed, and I said, I'm not kidding! You can't do this without knowing everyone's name at the bare minimum.

When you're a new principal, you need to get to know your people. You don't have to lay out all of your ideas or observations the first time you meet. You're much better off listening to theirs, anyway. You begin with connections. Then you develop a relationship that leads to trust, and *then* you become someone who can influence the way they think, which will lead to the way they act, and then the behaviors they choose as a part of this team.

By The Way, You Build Relationships In Order To...

You need to build relationships. This is one of those things that you've probably heard most everyone suggest that you need to do as a new principal. But, why?

When people find value in the work, they are more likely to enjoy it, to do well in it, and to be effective. In schools, the principal plays a big part (as we've mentioned) in how the adults see their job. People perform better when they think they're a part of a team that's on the move. We tend to raise (or lower) our game to the environment we're in. The principal embodies the vision, expectations, and focus of the school. You can't overestimate how important that role is in the performance of others. Leadership *really* matters because when it's good, others choose to commit at a higher level. When leadership is bad you get the opposite; your best people hold back their commitment until they believe that the leader has what it takes to bring it all together for success.

That's why you hear so much about relationships and leadership. What relationships do is give you a vehicle to differentiate what you have to share about vision, mission, purpose, and values to each of your people. The relationship makes it personal for your people… your skill as a communicator makes it effective.

So, you build relationships to be a part of a joint effort to provide a quality education for all of the children. You *don't* build relationships to have friends. You may not like that notion, and I suppose you can see it as cynicism, but that's not where it comes from. It comes from the posture that you are the leader of a group, doing a particular thing. As the leader, you bring others together to do the work; you will have to, if you're an effective leader, have hard conversations with those same people that you have built relationships with. You have to do both.

It doesn't mean that you don't build a great spirit of togetherness among the people of your school; you do. It means, however, that you have multiple roles to play. Bringing people together is one; evaluating them and holding them accountable for their work is another. It's the third bowl of porridge, yet again. So much of what you do in school leadership is looking for that *just right* combination, that sweet mid-range. Not too cold, not too hot…just right.

Jack Zenger and Joseph Folkman have researched leadership effectiveness for decades and have measured the impact of two leadership traits on performance: warmth and competence. Their work, including studying tens of thousands of case studies, suggests that the best of leaders combine both.

In my experience, I've seen leaders who *didn't* reach that balance. Those who are mostly warm with little competence can seem okay for a while, but over time the teachers (who want competent leadership) don't respond to someone who is lacking in knowledge or skills. The same is true in reverse. I've seen leaders who were very competent but lacked warmth who weren't successful for long as principals. The most effective principals have a balance of the two.

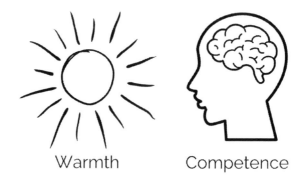

Warmth   Competence

I was coaching a new principal and asked him before the year began if he had yet determined what was the "big work" he needed to do right out of the gate. He replied, "oh yes! I am going to work on climate and when that's done I'll get to work on the real stuff."

My reply was, "what if climate *is* the real stuff?" It's the combination that makes school work... morale + expectations... order + space to learn... the individual + the whole group... and for the leader, *warmth + competence.* They are both *the real stuff.*

BUILD A TEAM

It is teamwork that remains the ultimate competitive advantage both because it is so powerful, and so rare.

~Patrick Lencioni

What is the best team you've ever been a part of? What made it a great team? Did you win something together? Were you particularly close? Did you overcome great odds to be successful? What made that one the best?

Who brought you together? How did they do it?

As the principal and as a leader, your mental models are built by your frame of reference. Chances are that having been part of the school world for a while, you've been on a lot of teams. One of the most important things you'll do as principal (that list seems to be getting longer...?!?) is to <u>bring a group of people together to do meaningful work.</u>

So, what have you learned in your experience about how that's done?

Building a team, bringing people together as a group working toward a goal or goals, is the best friend the principal could ever have. Here's why: you are always going to have more people to reach than time to do so. You *aren't* going to have adequate time to guide the behavior of your faculty and staff on your own. The good news? You don't have to. *The greatest influences on a teacher are the teachers who are in her hall, to her left, to her right, and across the hall.*

Environment has a powerful influence on behavior. If the people around you are committed to excellence, chances are you'll follow their lead. The same is true in reverse, however. If the people around you are committed to mediocrity, it takes a lot to stand alone.

If this sounds like a description of what culture is, it should. Culture can be defined as *the way we do things around here.* Team is the organizing device for building culture. It unites people and provides a setting in which, if curated appropriately by leadership, an opportunity to define the culture. But, it starts with "team."

So, how do you build a team at a school? There are a lot of ways, but all of them require *intent* and *time.* Teams don't automatically "happen." For example, if you put a group of individual teachers together in a grade-level team or a department, they don't just start working together as one after introductions. In fact, my experience has shown me that without intentional effort to bring them together, they are most likely to stay apart in some fashion.

That same group of educators, if given time and the intentional processes that lead to becoming a team, might be your best example of collaboration ever.

The same is true of partnerships at the school… counselors, assistant principals, paraprofessional and classroom teacher. How about a collaborative classroom? Partnering a special education teacher with a general ed teacher (often without common planning) doesn't reach the potential of what that team might be. If they spend time before and during their work together to become a team, they are more likely to work together as you had hoped.

What are these team-building activities? There are no specific "magical" activities that bring people together, but there are some frames on which they all seem to work best;

1. Time. For people to work together, they need to spend time together. What does time do? It builds **trust.** Which allows vulnerability. Which is a necessary ingredient for learning, and coming together as a team is very much a *learning exercise.*

2. Shared Purpose. People are willing to work with others when the *work is work worth doing.* It's why the effective leader keeps her team members in sight of their purpose for being there.

3. The In-Between. A student in one of my leadership classes shared this insight about becoming a team:

> "I played on basketball teams in college and professionally and we didn't become a team during the games. We didn't even become a team at practice. We became a team on bus rides, in hotel lobbies... we became a team during the in-between times."
>
> ~Antoine Whelchel

The in-between for us in the school world is a hard thing to get. We barely have time for what we're doing! Because of this, the effective team-builder dedicates time for activities that bring people together.

Principals everywhere have employed PLCs (Professional Learning Communities) as a part of their work. The PLCs that work the best are the ones that start at the right end first. Those who begin with *community* find the learning much more enjoyable and are more likely to engage in it. Those who go straight to the tasks without building the group together first often find that to be a missed step.

DON'T TRY TO DO EVERYTHING

A leader is best when people barely know he exists, when his work is done, his aim fulfilled, they will say: we did it ourselves.

~Lao Tzu

When you get a leadership position, particularly when you become the PRINCIPAL, you'll have to repress the urge to do everything. It comes at you from many angles.

1. <u>The Name on the Door.</u> When you're the principal, others will hold you accountable for everything that happens at the school. That alone causes many principals to be anxious about things happening at the school. You're not wrong... when you're the principal it ultimately comes back to you, but if your instinct is to try to do it all to avoid things going awry, you're probably going to be disappointed. And tired.

2. <u>Your Personality.</u> Many of the people who are attracted to school administration are high achievers. They value achievement and succeeding at a high level, higher than they value collaboration. This is NOT a bad thing on its own; ambition and competitiveness can be helpful for leaders when they are contained. If it keeps you from working with others though, it can leave the leader missing important facets of the job, and very tired.

3. <u>Memory of Getting Burned.</u> If you put your trust in someone or a group of someones and they didn't get the job

done, you may decide that it's not worth it to collaborate. ("See? Told you it would have been better just to do it on my own!") That previous negative experience may lead to trust issues. Here's the problem with that: you MUST have others trust you in order to be their leader. If people are anything, a lot of them are very perceptive when it comes to emotions. If they feel (or see) you not trust them, they are unlikely to trust you.

A lot of reasons/explanations for the principal to try to do it all on her own.

Here's the case for collaborating:

1. <u>Doing it yourself will burn you out.</u> This isn't opinion; this one's fact. There are too many things that have to be done for you to do them on your own. Getting yourself wrapped up in minutiae isn't the role of the principal. You need some space… some distance from the action… in order to see the bigger picture. You certainly spend time at ground level, but your job uniquely requires you to zoom in and zoom out.

2. <u>It's not sustainable.</u> Here's something I learned *after* I had finished my years of being the principal, and I've worked to get the principals I teach to understand it: what YOU do exclusively has less of a chance to keep going after you're gone than things that you did COLLABORATIVELY. If you really love something and make it "your baby", it is an at-risk idea when you leave, because no one has the ownership needed to champion the idea. When your people are involved in not only the implementation but the <u>creation </u>of ideas, they are more likely to keep them moving on when you have moved on.

3. It's not your job to do everything. Your job is to teach others what and how. If they only come there to watch you work, they aren't going to learn either.

Here's a way to check yourself (before you wreck yourself, shoutout to Ice Cube):
- each month, pick a day, make a chart of what you do, (please see a sample below)
- conduct an audit of your choices.
    - If you are doing things other people could do, it's time to develop a strategy to share those things.
    - What important things are you missing? There are certain things that only the principal can do.
    - When you fill your time with other things, you'll look busy, but you might not be as effective as you need to be.

CHOICE Audit

Name _____ Date _____

Time	Activity	Only the Principal	Someone Else

- Whenever you choose to DO something, you simultaneously choose to NOT DO something;
- Please list some of the high impact, principal-only actions you chose to not do today.

Actions I Chose NOT To Do Today

When you write it down (which seems to be more effective than typing it but either will be better than not doing it) you have to come to terms with the choices you've made. If you do it with authenticity, you'll be able to self-correct some habits that you may have developed or some choices you're making that aren't the most effective.

Work Choices

DO   DIRECT   DELEGATE   DON'T DO

If you're thinking, "sure, but if I don't do it, it won't get done," let's get back to the nature of your role. You are there for leadership… which is by definition you + others. This isn't a suggestion that you don't get things done… but a plea that you don't try to do them all yourself.

For all of the actions that come into your space each day, you have choices in how to respond. It's not *only* a binary Do or Not Do… you also have choices to Direct and to Delegate.

Direct is *Delegate Lite.* You still keep the authority but you include others in the task, directing them in specific tasks of which they are responsible. It's *better* than you doing it all, and better than it not getting done, but it is still limiting. It takes a lot of your head space and oxygen, AND because you keep the accountability to yourself, the others don't learn how to perform under the stress or how to adapt to make something work. There are some things at the school that you will always choose to direct; that's a good thing as long as you aren't stopping there.

Delegate. You do, you do together, they do. Teach someone how to do, and then let them hold the accountability and do the learning. Where people get this wrong is by thinking they can start with someone with minimal experience doing a maximum stakes job. Delegation is not dereliction of duty! You don't just pass things over without clarity of purpose and vision of success. But, you begin to grow capacity by getting others to be in charge of things.

You may be thinking"this book has a lot about figuring out your job." Yes. I've worked with hundreds of principals, I also have personal experience from my own career as principal. I wish I'd had this understanding while I was a principal. I did some empowerment, but some of the things I loved the most, I kept my hands on. I inadvertently decreased their chances of becoming sustainable by not involving more people not only in their implementation, but in their design and creation.

YOUR ASSISTANT PRINCIPAL(S)

Don't mess with the bull, young man.
You'll get the horns.

~Richard Vernon
Assistant Principal
Shermer High School , 1985

When you are the principal, your most significant professional relationship is the one you have with your assistant principal or assistant principals. Among the hundreds of principals I've delivered executive coaching to, the most common thread among those who have struggled has been *assistant principal issues.* That's not to say that it's the AP who is to blame when the principal doesn't make it; often there are AP problems and the principal is the one who is at fault for not having been proactive in their work with the AP.

Your AP is your acolyte… taking the light of your vision to share with the people of the school. When done well, it lights the school with possibility. When done poorly, it can burn the place down.

If you brought twenty APs together from different schools, chances are they would have twenty different stories of what they do in their jobs. The role of AP is often situational based on the needs of the school, the system, and the principal. One thing that ALL twenty should be doing is spreading the vision and values across the school. Doing what the principal wants them to do in the manner in which they want it done.

Remember, you can't do it all when you're the principal. What makes a school a place of consistent excellence is when the people who work there are on the same page, and that page represents a vision and values that can light the path to success. In order to do that, the principal needs to elevate the conversation to help others understand HOW they should approach their work.

This is where the relationship you have with your assistant principal(s) becomes key. The teachers and staff look at all of you as *administration*. It's critical that the administrators sing from the same page of music. When school is running at its best, a teacher could ask the principal and the assistant principal the same question and get the same response delivered in a similar tone.

Consistency. If you have it, your teachers and students know what to expect and that gives them confidence. If you *don't* have it, it causes a number of potential problems. Some teachers will keep asking different administrators a question until they find an admin who gives them the answer they're looking for. If you're building an equitable school and workplace, consistency is important.

When you're the principal, you want your APs above everyone else to make decisions based on the same values you're making decisions from. You should be continually teaching your APs about your core values. Find ways to say it that they can understand and then repeat to the people they interact with at the school. These are things that you want everyone to value, so it's critical that the first adopters be your assistant principals.

Your work with your APs doesn't end with sharing a list of things of which they're in charge. What seems to cause more difficulty than *what* to do is *how* to do it.

A principal I was working with had two assistant principals. One primarily worked in "discipline" and spent time with students and their parents. The other AP focused on instruction and spent most of her time with the teachers. I visited the principal in August and asked her how everything was and she was full of energy and excitement and bouncing around the room.

I came back in September and she was delayed in meeting with me as she needed to finish a meeting with a teacher. I asked her how things were going and she was positive but much less enthusiastic. Then I asked her how she was spending her time and she said with teachers. And with parents.

By the time I returned in October, her head was cradled in her arms, resting on her desk looking shell shocked. I asked her how things were going and she sort of mumbled fine… everything is fine. I asked her how she was spending her time and she said *I'm spending all of my time smoothing over things that my APs have done. They keep making everybody mad and I have to follow up to keep it from being worse.*

So I asked her, what are you doing or not doing now compared to when things were going well in August? She said a few things, and I asked what's different now for your APs.

She thought about it for a minute and said, we aren't meeting as much as we were at the beginning of the year. I said, okay, that's helpful. When is the last time you met to get on the same page… not logistics and who is covering what event, but when is the last time you spent time to teach them *how* you want them to do their work.

Her head fell forward and she said, August.

I said, you mean August, when you were happy and everything was going well?

From my experience, if you're the principal, you need to meet with your APs every week. Sure, you'll see them in the hallways and at duty, but when you *plan* to meet with them, they get to ask you *how* you would have done things. You get to inquire as to how they made the decisions they made. You get to reinforce your priorities and revalidate your core values.

When you can communicate what you're after, meet regularly to review how it's going and what questions have arisen, you have gone into teaching mode and without it, you're just hoping they figure it out. Sometimes they do! But not all of the time.

Here's an example from one of the schools I led. I believe that if you treat people with respect and kindness you influence their response for the better. If you hassle people, they feel like they aren't important and that too influences how they interact with you.

Among my APs, support staff, and other administrative types, in our regular meetings I emphasized *at our school we don't hassle people.* Schools certainly need rules and have to have order, but I've seen some that seem to pride themselves on having DMV vibes for all interactions. What if we tried to get people what they wanted instead? Would that change the way they think about us and the school?

I know this about school and really all organizations: *what gets talked about gets done. What gets frequently examined gets done well.*

We intentionally focused on making our school as *hassle free* as we possibly could. There was a form certifying a student's attendance they needed to get in order to get their driver's license. When I arrived, students and their parents were told they needed to get their request in a week in advance before they needed it. We changed it to… same day service. We had to embrace the attitude before we could make the change. And to do that, we had to say *"we don't hassle people"* so frequently that it became true.

As we've mentioned before, there are SO many moving parts to a school. As the leader, you assess where you are, what you need, and then communicate it constantly. Doing so with your APs is essential; they are your hands, your feet, and your eyes throughout the school.

Make certain they understand *how* you want things done. If they aren't doing what you're doing in the manner in which you want it done, consider that an assessment that guides instruction. Then develop your strategies for helping them better understand. Meet every week to *listen* to them. Be specific in what you ask. For example, *in what ways did you hassle anyone this week?* Then, *in what ways did you handle things differently?*

Again, you have to pick things to focus on that will really matter for your school and your people. You can't have ten, twenty, thirty points of emphasis at a time. Approach this as you approached your job as a classroom teacher. You never would have tried to teach everything to everybody all at one time. You started with your instructional goals and *then* developed a scope and sequence. You built your unit and lesson plans, your instructional strategies, your assessments, your remediation and your enrichment.

This principal thing? Same deal. Your students? All of the adults. If you want their behaviors and choices to align with your values and priorities, you're going to need to hit "teacher mode." The good news? You KNOW HOW to do this!

As you teach your Assistant Principals, you are simultaneously developing a train-the-trainer model. They take what they learn from you and cascade it through the school.

What often DOESN'T work is to assume your AP knows enough already, can "work the duty list" you share with them, and do it like you would do it. That's what leads to a bad feeling in October. If you are spending your time cleaning up messes and missteps from your APs, you aren't doing the job of principal. And, it's not their fault if you don't emphasize priorities and teach to the level of understanding with them.

You spend more time teaching your APs than you do with anyone else because you leverage them to get to the others. Think about it like this… you are the water tower, and you flow through the main lines (your APs and other administrative types) to get to the service lines (your teachers) who carry the water to the tap. That's where the students drink from. Not from the water tower. For you to get things where they need to go, you need to use gravity and keep the water flowing through the pipes. If you get stopped at the main lines (your APs) nobody is getting any water. What this is all about is you not being the point of impact for most of your students (direct contact) but for you to *flow through* the people of your school to reach everybody. And that is what we call influence.

… it's how you say it. When you become principal, you typically have had experience as assistant principal in which you learned *how to say it.* (I'm assuming you learned how to say it since you got the principal job!) Your APs? They may not yet know *how* to say it. When you send them off on their journey without instructions, without observations, without feedback, you are just hoping they already know how or they quickly learn *how* to say it.

There's not much that's more important. When you are a school administrator, you sit in a seat of authority before whomever you're working with, be it parents, students, or teachers. Do your APs already have the skillset to adapt how they talk to each of the groups? Do your APs come off as professional? Arrogant? Unprepared? Respectful?

I would think that this is something that matters a lot to you. Usually you find out in arrears that things are going great when those interactions are followed up by a call to you. What if you spent prepared time (like you were a teacher, remember) and created scenarios with your AP(s)? What if you used role play to help guide their growth? What if you brought one of your trusted teachers in to be a part of the role play?

These strategies and more can help you better train your AP on *how* to say it. This will give them confidence, give you an idea of their competence level in interpersonal conversations, and demonstrate to your AP that you're committed to their growth.

CHANGE

Don't ever take down a fence until you know the reason why it was put up.

~G.K. Chesterton

You're the new principal! You're excited, ready to get going at your new school and you just feel like you want to change something! But, everyone has said be careful what you change. So what can you change? When can you change it?

First, let's take a look at change to get a clear perspective of what you're up against. Elizabeth Kubler-Ross identified the five stages of grief in her 1969 book *On Death and Dying*. Those stages of the grief cycle are familiar to us now– Denial, Anger, Bargaining, Depression, and Acceptance. Her original focus was on death and loss, but over time many practitioners and academics alike noticed that the five stages of grief seemed to be on target for the *stages of change*. So much so that the EKR Foundation adapted the five original stages into an updated version entitled the Kubler-Ross Change Curve.

Change by many estimations is a loss, and a loss requires grief so it shouldn't surprise us that the emotional process of accepting change fits with the Kubler-Ross curve.

For school leaders, often billed as "change agents," there is a formidable emotional process that comes with any efforts to make change. Depending on the change, the depth of emotional response varies. I've been around schools that were closing. The level of grieving is high when a school closes, particularly for those who have invested years there. Smaller changes don't necessarily bring the heightened response to everyone involved, but don't underestimate even small changes. To someone, the new way represents two things that can evoke intense emotional response: loss and the unknown.

For the new or newer principal, the unknown can be particularly challenging when bringing about change. They are just at that moment processing the change in leadership of which you are a part. You are unknown when you begin (even if you've worked there before, you're unknown as principal). When you are a known and **trusted** quantity, the unknown often isn't as emotional and the greatest issue of the change is the loss itself.

Said simply, if you're early in your tenure and you bring about change, more emotions are attached than if you've been there long enough to earn trust and influence thinking.

What you choose to change then is best selected in areas that affect a small enough number of people whose emotions you can manage until they reach a level of acceptance. Changing your grading policies in year one? Too soon. Changing how we do graduation, the prom, or other traditions? Too many people – your whole community –are involved in those things. Changing the parent pickup line at an elementary school? Wouldn't it be better to talk to the parents first before you change things? You might learn an even better idea than the one you have. Additionally, people are less emotional about the change they helped develop.

It's not that we don't like emotions… it's that as the principal you spend a lot of time *explaining* things. If you are able to do so in a conversation based on logic, it's much easier. The deeper that conversation is grounded in emotions, the harder it is to have.

This nearly-magical thing happens when things go right. *OVER TIME* (not immediately) people develop trust and confidence in you as the leader. That trust speeds up their time in the stages of grief/change. See what happened there? We DO like emotions... We just like the ones that are based on trusting you more than we like the ones that don't! So what day is that on the calendar for you? It depends on a number of factors... how primed for change your faculty and staff are ... your ability to connect with them... your efforts to influence their opinion of you before they develop one on their own.

Never doubt that a small group of thoughtful, committed people can change the world. Indeed. It is the only thing that ever has.

~Margaret Mead

You should know it when you get there. If nothing else, you'll know you're *not* there yet if you try to bring about change and it flops.

Again, for clarification, it's not like you're waiting on a bus to arrive. You have to be doing things during these days to *earn* trust...to gain their permission to be their leader... for them to be confident in you that you are who you say you are and you mean them no harm (and might even mean them well!) Those things are... spending time with your people, asking them questions, *listening* to them.

BEING SUCCESSFUL AS THE PRINCIPAL

The key to student success is a great school and the key to a great school is a great principal.

~NASSP and NAESP

Around 25,000 principals separate from their school at the end of each year, leaving schools in constant states of turnover. Around half of all school principals depart their school by the end of their third year, and only about one out of four high school principals make it through year five.

We are in a state of principal churn, and our schools and students are the ones who feel the negative effects. The principal is attributed to about 25% of the school's impact on student achievement and the most effective principals are worth months of learning to the average student at their school. Leadership matters and we have lots of turnover in the position across the country.

What makes the difference? Here are seven reasons why principals are successful… or they struggle.

1. Preparation. There are three performance dimensions to the principal's job: knowledge, skills, and dispositions. When the leader is prepared in each of those three areas good things are going to happen. When there is a hole in any or all of those areas, however, it often comes to light quickly. The principals who are able to be successful in the job are better prepared for it; those who struggle get to the

job without being ready for it either because of lacking skill sets (able to bring others together to work effectively), knowledge base (unfamiliar with special education laws, lack of familiarity with curriculum), or leadership dispositions (not able to relate to others, failure to build relationships)

2. Communication. Principals who are effective communicators are able to spread the vision and help others improve in their work. They are good listeners first and are skillful in motivating teachers and staff to do their best.

3. Leading. Principals have to be able to have tough conversations. They have to be willing to make decisions for the best of the school and the students even when they know that it won't make everyone happy. The most effective leaders are able to get others to join them in the journey to success. Struggling leaders try to do it all alone.

4. Judgment. Everyone is assessing you as a leader in three categories: your judgment, your treatment of others, and your results. Often if your results are good, your judgment will be considered good as well, but if your results are faltering your judgment will come into question. How do you have good judgment? Through experience. You either gain that by making your own mistakes or by trusting others who have made them in their experience. It's good to listen.

5. Confidence. Just as students can smell fear in a new teacher or a substitute, the teachers can tell whether you are a confident leader or not. Those who are doubting themselves give room for others to doubt them as well. Too much confidence is a problem as well, but not enough is worse. People don't want to follow those who aren't strong enough to lead.

6. Time Management. Time management is hard on everyone. The truth is, this job is going to take more of it than you have. So, it's not about that, but rather about

knowing what has to be done and then getting to what should be done. The most effective principals utilize staff and are experts in delegating. Those who tend to micromanage and are controllers have difficulty in leadership positions.

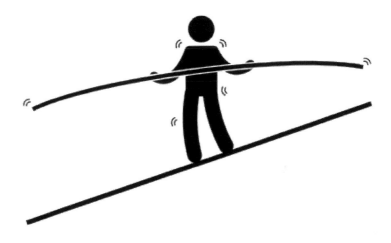

7. Balance. Connected with time management is balance. Principals who work too much and are preoccupied with their jobs think they're doing what they're supposed to do, but either burn out, crash, or lose their effectiveness. The most effective principals have a hobby, spend time with family and friends regularly, and are able to give their brains the space and time needed to process all of the work they do the rest of the time.

8. Support Network. For new principals, the winning formula is: 1:1 leadership coaching on a regular basis; regular and consistent participation in a cohort of peers; real-time feedback from the supervisor of principals throughout the year; and finally, a supportive environment from the system level.

STARTING THE YEAR WITH YOUR FACULTY AND STAFF

If you want to build a ship, don't drum up people to collect wood and don't assign them tasks and work , but rather teach them to long for the endless immensity of the sea.
~Antoine de Saint Exupery

While I was at dinner, I heard someone in the restaurant, obviously a teacher, talking to a friend in line. I heard her reply, but context leads me to believe it was the question every teacher hears in late Summer.

"Are you about ready for school to start?"

The teacher replied back, "yes, I'm excited to get back to the kids and to have a routine, but I'll miss my summer! We will go back next week."

So, before your teachers return to school, they're thinking about it. And others are asking them about it.

For you as the school leader, it's a time you should be excited about. These teachers are your stars; they are the ones who will lead your students to discovery, to curiosity, to knowledge. You should be as excited for them to return to you as the parents are to send their children back to you and your teachers.

As you prepare for the beginning of the school year,, here are **Ten Things To Remember** about teachers and their return to school.

1. **<u>Help All Your Teachers Get Off To An Inspired Start.</u>**
    You can tell them all of the rules they'll ever need to know
    on the first day you have them back, or you can get them
    excited about what they do and the promise of a new year.
    Which method leads to instructional success?
2. **<u>Teach your teachers what you want them to know; don't
    just tell them.</u>** It's easy for you to look at the list of things
    you want your teachers to know, and the short time you
    have them to yourself and to try to tell them too much.
    Does it really serve you (or them) well for you to try to
    cover more things than they can digest? The school year
    lasts a while; you don't <u>really</u> need to tell them everything
    at once.
3. **<u>Together, Design a Great First Day With Students.</u>**
    What one thing do you want your teachers to focus on in
    preparation for their first day with their students? If you
    take *your* time with them to prepare them for that goal, will
    the beginning of school go smoothly? Are you clear in
    your description of what you want the first days with
    students to be? Painting that picture is important if you
    want your expectations to be met. Taking the time to get
    the FDOS (First Day of School) right will pay dividends all
    year long.
4. **<u>Atmosphere Contributes to Performance</u>.** If your first
    days with your teachers seem rushed, over-scheduled, and
    full of tension, that will set a tone that you may not mean to
    set. What if you and your administrative team met your
    teachers as they entered the school on the first day? Giving
    them high-fives and fist bumps like you'd like them to do
    when *their* students arrive? If you model this, would it be
    more impactful than if you merely told them?
5. **<u>Define the Focus for the Year.</u>** A few years ago, I heard
    some nice, wonderful school leaders tell their faculty what
    the focus would be for the upcoming year. They then
    unveiled a powerpoint presentation for over an hour and

shared **Fourteen Areas of Focus** for the upcoming year!!! My expectations for their success are... very guarded. If you tell your team fourteen things are important, they may not *actually* focus on the one that really *is* the most important. Please don't say 'priority' if you don't mean it.

6. <u>**Give Your Teachers Space and Time to Connect with Each Other.**</u> Your teachers will be working together, collaboratively, this year. Don't forget to give them time to connect and build trust with each other during the first days of school.

7. <u>**Give Special Attention To Your New Teachers.**</u> Who on your administrative team will advocate for each of the new teachers on your staff? Sure, they have a faculty mentor, but on your team, who will shepherd each of them through the first days? If you are checking in on them (in person) a couple of times each day during pre-planning and the first days, you'll set the tone that you aren't going to leave their success to chance and that you are going to be there for them.

8. <u>**Be Rested and Ready for the Teachers' First Day**</u>. Here's an idea worthy of your consideration: do all of the planning for your teachers' return, and on the night before they arrive, get refreshed for the next day. (Exercise, walk, do something non-school; then get a good night's sleep) Before you start shaking your head "NO!", hear me out, please: You have to stop your preparation for the teachers' return sometime. Stop it with enough time to get yourself to *<u>your best</u>* as they arrive. If you are full of energy that first day, you set the tone in a good way. If you are dragging on their first day, it'll do the opposite.

9. <u>**Focus on the Good.**</u>   Chances are that most of what you plan for the teachers' first day will go well... but chances are something may not go as you planned. This is a time when your teachers will see how you respond in such a scenario. Is it better for them to see you adapt gracefully or

to respond fretfully to the unplanned or unexpected? If the food for breakfast arrives later than you planned, you *can* let it ruin your day, or you can keep your focus on the good. And there's lots of good on the first day for teachers.

10. **Take Time for Your People.** Will your school get off to a better start with you getting around the building and seeing all of your people on their first day(s) back? How you spend your time on those first days shows others *your* focus, and the winning hand in school leadership is always a focus on leading your teachers.

Teachers Appreciate Organization and Good Management of Time

Time. The problem for every principal, particularly at the beginning of the year. During this season, it's reasonable for you to be saying that you don't have enough time for all of the things you want to share with your teachers before school begins. The truth is, you don't. So, what's next?

Many leaders do what they've seen in the past and forsake good teaching to their teachers to make sure that they "cover" everything that has to be covered before the year begins. A reasonable question to ask is this:

> *What that you share during pre-planning is* actually *being heard by your teachers? Of that, what is being understood? And of that subset, what will they be able to effectively incorporate in their practice?*

Not to make you feel bad, but if you **say** everything that's on your list, but they either don't **hear** or **understand,** or if they aren't able to **transfer the information**, what have you really accomplished?

Adult learners need to process their thoughts out loud with colleagues in order to enhance the likelihood of understanding. Standing up increases brain activity by **five percent.** (Walking gives you a **fifteen percent** boost). Consider pausing to let your learners "mindshare" **at least every ten minutes.**

What's the solution? Here are some practical, real-life things you can do as your teachers return and you get them ready for the year to make this time well-spent.

1. During your time with your faculty, **check for understanding frequently.** If you are giving your faculty a series of things you want them to know, <u>consider:</u>
    1. pausing after each item, or at least after each set of items, ask them to share their understanding with the person sitting next to them; asking them to stand up is a good thing during this as well;
    2. ask some of them to share with the whole group; (consider asking three of your team to share; always have a person to serve as the timer other than you so answers will be as brief as you want them)
    3. acknowledge your team's processing of the learning and reteach as needed to get to understanding.
2. Plan your pre-planning work with your teachers just like they say to pack for a big trip: **lay it all out and then only take half of it with you.** Think about it like this: if you could only share one thing, what would it be? How about two? What is the maximum number of items that you can share that *you can be confident your teachers will be able to operationalize or act on?* You really don't have to tell them everything at once and if you did they wouldn't remember it. What do you do with the rest of what you want to tell them? (See number three below!)
3. Your bookkeeper comes to the faculty meeting before the year begins and tells everyone how to take up money for a fundraiser. She talks about not leaving checks overnight in a desk; she tells them to write receipts; she asks them to not bring a bunch of change from the penny drive in at 4:15 on

a Friday. Fast forward to February. Someone has a fundraiser. It's been six months since they were told how to do it. They do it all wrong. What is a better way to get this info to others? Videos. Technology.

> **What if you built a library of short (3-4 minute) videos to show your teachers "How To..." do the things you'd like them to do?** What if they went to that shared Google Drive **when** they needed to know things and it was there, waiting for them? There's really no end to the good you can do by building your "How To" video library for your teachers. You can ask some of your all-star teachers to make brief videos on how to effectively call parents, working with struggling students, or even how to effectively utilize group learning. You can make a 3-4 minute video about... whatever you want your teachers to know throughout the year. In-Time learning is better than in-case learning every day of the week. (NOTE: these videos don't have to be produced-- they can be made with phones. AND, you don't have to be the star of all of them (some of them you will want to be). Collect and curate the collective knowledge of "How To" do things at your school and you will have effectively given yourself time.

You can easily use a number of platforms to curate videos "made by your school, just for your school" that can save EVERYONE tons of time. How to "do grades"? Use a screencast to show them how.

Use the summer to meticulously plan for your teachers' return to school and you'll reap the dividends of a good start. That plan should be about doing fewer things better than nothing really great.

JOY

The way that I see it,
if you want the rainbow
you gotta put up with the rain.

~Dolly Parton

I love school.

I love the first day of school. And Homecoming Week. I love door holders and line leaders. I love kindergartners in Art class. I love elementary chorus and sixth grade band. I love ROTC and Drama. I love basketball and baseball, science labs and poetry slams.

I love rectangle pizza. With corn, a donut, and chocolate milk. Sometimes I order that at our local pizza place and they look at me funny.

I love being at an elementary school where the kids wave at you and think you're a big deal even though they don't know who you are.

I love middle schoolers and how they change…not just over time, but during the day. If they're mad at you, stand by… they may like you again before 3:30.

I love a good alternative school that focuses on second chances and possibilities.

I love high school. I love the awkwardness of freshmen and the potential of high school seniors.

I love teachers. Teachers should have special parking everywhere they go. They should get free coffee at fast food places and a donut every Friday from Krispy Kreme and Dunkin.

I love that teachers know that it's not easy but they do it anyway. I love it when they get right to the edge of giving up or giving in but they don't. I love that they get Christmas presents. I love it when they have moments they wouldn't exchange for rubies and emeralds.

I love coaches, especially the ones who are at tiny schools coaching things they never played so that the kids at that school can have a team. And making 47 cents an hour to do it.

I love that so much of what we do at school is just doing nice things for other people. Like when the teachers of a small rural school have a homecoming dance in the cafeteria so their students can have something nice.

I love all of the details that happen at schools. All of the special touches and little things.

I love it when a teacher notices that one of her students needs something and finds some way for them to get it, but without any fanfare about it.

I love field trips. To see a child's eyes when they see something for the first time in real life. When their world expands exponentially because their teachers thought enough of them to do all the things to make a field trip happen.

I love that school can be hard. It has to be for it to mean something.

I love learning. Curiosity. Wonder. Awe.

What a wonderful gift to be in a profession that allows us to put our arms around people when they're having their worst day and to put our hands together for them when they have their best days. When I'm traveling, I get excited when I see a school like I've seen a historic site or the world's largest ball of yarn. I think about what's happened there and what is happening there. It always makes me smile.

When I think about school, I think about joy. I suppose I could think about other things, and it would be fair to do so, but I choose joy. And that makes all the difference.

Part II. In Your Head

THE POWER OF YOU

Life is pure adventure, and the sooner we realize that, the sooner we will be able to treat life as art.

~Maya Angelou

When a new school year begins, it's important for the principal and the administrative team to focus on the mindset of the teachers as they prepare to welcome the students for another year of exploration and learning.

Here is an activity you can use that can help connect your teachers to their purpose, to their colleagues, to the school's vision, and to their work this year.

<u>Life Maps.</u> As you look out at the faculty you've assembled, it's important to consider that they are unquestionably the greatest resource you have to accomplish the good work of the school. So, what drives them? What path led them to be a part of your school? What are their anchors?

Consider leading your faculty in an exploration of their journey by asking them to draw their life maps. (Remember "the Game of Life"? Twisting, turning, full of curves and traps.) It's a simple exercise: Give your teachers each a sheet of chart paper, some sharpies, and ask them to search google images for 'life maps' , not for a template but for some inspiration in designing their own map.

They'll need adequate time to reflect on their lives... their choices, their triumphs, their tragedies, and the essential points in their journey that led them to your school. (This is probably a thirty-minute event).

After they've finished their maps, depending upon the size of your team, you have several options for your teachers to share the story of their journey. You can break them up into small groups (6-8 is what we've learned works best) and ask each person to share their story. Then, you can ask *all* of your faculty to post their maps in a hallway or room for a gallery walk. As your teachers walk around and look at their colleagues' journeys, give them post-it notes so they can make comments as they make their way around. (Sort of an Instagram, alpha version!)

What can you hope to get from this exercise? For all of the groups I've used this with, the individuals in the group have discovered a deep appreciation for the other members of their cohort. Even at schools where the faculty has been together for a number of years, I'm amazed at how important parts of someone's life has seemed to remain unknown by other colleagues.

This is more than an ice-breaker or a get-to-know-you activity. WHO your people really are (and what experiences led them to this point) has a significant impact on HOW they work with others, and WHAT they will do each day in their work. When your faculty members get to know each other and appreciate their paths, it breaks down walls, gives them a point on which to connect, and opens the door to deep collaboration.

Your school will be more effective if your faculty works collaboratively and with respect for one another. As they learn more about each other and the paths that led them together, they have a greater likelihood of coming together to do extraordinary work with their students.

And if you arrive there, it was well worth the investment of time.

Method:

1. Distribute a piece of chart paper to each member of your faculty. Give them adequate table space to create their map. (Note: Everyone completes their own map, but they may want options for this activity. Offer choice to your learners. Some might want to work in the same space as a colleague to talk while they work; others might need quiet.)
2. Based on your group size (leadership team? whole faculty? departments or grade levels?), determine if you'll have your teachers share their journey with the whole group or in smaller groups.
3. Consider posting the maps in a gallery style and give everyone post-it notes to "leave comments" on other's maps.
4. Ask your teachers to reflect. You can do this in a written format, or you may choose to do a stand-up rotation for dialogue. Some questions for reflection could include:
   1. How does the path that led you to this point impact who you are as a teacher?
   2. What did you learn about your colleagues through this activity?
   3. Why do the journeys of you and your colleagues matter in the work of your school?
   4. What's next in your journey?
5. You may have other variables you want to add to this activity, but one of the biggest take-aways most groups have is how applicable it is to their classroom and with their students. Getting to know your students and the journey they have been on is also an important pathway to their success.

CONFIDENCE

Your success will be determined by your own confidence and fortitude.

~Michelle Obama

What if you had *bubble vision*? What if you could see people's thought bubbles as they walked by you each day? I'm thinking this would be one of the worst super-powers you could ever have. I am pretty sure you would have some hurt feelings pretty much every day.

But if you could see what is going on inside the minds of your teachers, your students, your staff, you would have an idea of what they bring with them into your learning environment. Would you treat people differently if you knew what roads they were traveling? Would you better know how to support them in their work, in their learning? Could you see their insecurities and understand their behaviors more clearly?

That's a piece that would be of great value: knowing everyone's confidence level. Our confidence or our insecurities have a lot to do with our approach to any task, to learning, to school. It's one of the greatest wishes we can have for our graduates: confidence. With it, you can take on new challenges that you haven't faced before. Without it, many things seem insurmountable.

As the leader of the school, be confident. There are many things that you might feel insecure about. Maybe you face feelings that you're not good enough. That you don't know enough about instruction. Or special education law. Or how to help people resolve conflicts. Or any of another thousand things you encounter as a school principal. It's easy to be overwhelmed and feel like you missed something in your training or preparation. It's easy to think back on times that you failed. It's easy to slip into your insecurities.

But don't stay there. Rise up. Be courageous enough to be confident. Believe in yourself and in your work. Don't get arrogant. (School people almost always are extremely annoyed by arrogance and by arrogant people, so keep your humility blended with your confidence, please.) Be confident that the people you learned from taught you enough to lead. Be confident of your strengths and buoyed by your failures, which more than most anything brought you to where you are. Be faithful and full of faith. Faithful to the work and full of faith that you will be able to meet the challenges.

If you want a school with confident teachers, confident students, and a sense of optimism and positivity, let it begin with you. And let it begin every day. Seize your morning. Don't let the first thing you do each day be a dive into the bad. Stay out of that email until you've started your day off in a positive direction with prayer, meditation, and/or mindfulness. Get yourself together and cast the day in a positive light. Starting your day positively is as easy as 1-2-3.

68

<u>Today, I Will Focus On ...</u>

One thing that gives me hope for the day;

Two things I will accomplish today;

Three people whom I will seek to support today.

1-2-3. Think about it. Write about it. START in the right frame of mind and your day can continue with confidence. If you choose to go to email first, what is it that you're looking for? Problems. Look, they'll be there whether you seize your day first or let it seize you. It's a choice. Choose positive. 1-2-3.

With your mind in the right place, you are ready to begin the day. Confidently. On your way to work, don't get caught up in the churn of things. Continue your positive thinking. Play your "get psyched for school playlist." Make sure you get to your *walk-out* song before you get to school. You should always have a walk-out song, and it can change at different times of your life, different moods you're in, different times of the year. It's the song they would play if you were walking up to bat in the Major Leagues, or coming down the ramp to the ring in WWE. Your theme song. Your walk-out song.

That's what needs to be playing when you roll up into school every morning. Loud. Keep your sunglasses on. Pop out of that car and start strutting, keeping your song playing

69

in your head. (Chances are you're one of the first ones at school, so you may be strutting to yourself, but strut anyway.) Walk into school every morning like you're going to do something. Like you've got some hope about you. Like there are two things you're going to rock today, like there are three people who you're going to ignite today. Like you're going to do something. We are in the *"do something"* business. It's easier if you act like it.

Start with confidence and watch it spread. When you find others to ignite, to challenge, to bring joy to, it'll spread. When you get your two main goals accomplished by lunch, you'll be feeling like a rockstar. And hold onto that hope all day long. Confidence doesn't create a force field for life's challenges, but it does give you a different posture when they come your way. Strong. Capable. Resilient. Confident.

By The Way, Don't Be Afraid.

There are many things to be afraid of and about in school leadership. Work to replace your fears with confidence. I'm not talking about cautions and safety protocols; those aren't fears, those are critical parts of your job to be accomplished confidently. The fears of leadership to avoid are typically the more personal ones. Being afraid you don't know everything you need to know. (You don't) Being afraid you are going to encounter things that you haven't prepared for. (You will) Being afraid of being wrong. (You get a chance to do this most every day)

Don't equate confidence with recklessness. They aren't the same. What paralyzes school leaders quite often is a fear of *failure.* You'll gain confidence with time and success. On the way there, bolster your confidence by calling your mentors/coaches to be a sounding board for the most challenging situations. Replace fear with planning. Believe in you.

FOUNDATION

Effective leaders are made, not born.
They learn from trial and error,
and from experience.

~Colin Powell

One of the questions that often comes up about leadership is this one: **are leaders born or can leaders be made?**

Nearly every day, I think about leadership. I've been doing so for as long as I can remember. I'd been given "leadership opportunities" since I was very young.

Here's what I've come to believe: we all have the capacity to lead; we all have the capacity to learn to lead more effectively. To support that work, there is foundational work that should be done. With the foundation set, you are able to lead in the busy, unpredictable and unscripted world of school leadership. Without the foundation, it's easy to flounder, to float, and to not be prepared for the moments that need a leader.

Questions In Developing Your Leadership Foundation

1. ***Who Am I?*** At the core of leadership is self-awareness. One of the most important tools you'll use to grow as a leader is reflection, so getting a baseline is critical. Even more so, if you know who you are up front, it will be easier for you to keep yourself and avoid getting lost.
2. ***What Am I Here For?*** Purpose. What's your purpose? What is your mission? As the leader, what are you to do? Establishing your **personal vision and mission** is a

71

fundamental piece of leadership. If you are an aspiring leader, this is something you work on while you're in your preparation phase. If you have this established, you can hit the ground running when you assume your post as a school administrator.

3. ***What Do I Believe?*** In addition to identifying who you are and what you're here for, the leader is well-served by developing a **list of beliefs** pertinent to leadership. Making your belief statement is a perfect complement to your identity, your vision, and your mission. These are things you think to establish your true North and to serve as a compass for you in your work.

4. ***What Will I Fight For?*** This is typically a subset of your beliefs statement. In answering *"what will I fight for,"* you identify your deepest beliefs and strongest passions. These are the things that will be at the core of your work and will drive your actions on a daily basis. (I'm not a fan of the phrase "non-negotiable"... sounds a little too argumentative for the kind of leaders the school needs. Answering this question may seem similar, but it is a deeper commitment than even that. It's a basis for what you'll seek to do at your school as the leader. The sooner you establish this, the more focused you can be in your work.)

These questions aren't just an exercise or busywork. They are the fundamental base for you, who you are, and what you believe. Think about them. Write them down. **Update them at least annually.**

As you grow as a leader, some of your answers will stay the same and remain with you throughout your career. You'll add some things; you'll delete some things. That's part of what it means to grow.

ROADBLOCKS

The obstacle in the path becomes the path. Never forget within every obstacle is an opportunity to improve our condition.

~Ryan Holliday

One of the questions I often pose to leaders who I am coaching is this: *what stands between your school and success?* And, on the personal level: *what is blocking your path to success?*

You can't draw a map for your journey to success without beginning with "you are here." It's not always the most joyous thing to do, but if you can find the humility and vulnerability necessary to do so, it can be the step you need to move toward success.

We all carry things with us that can impede us from being successful. Some of them are personality traits that you didn't just pick up overnight... they are probably curated over many years and aren't easy to shed. Remember, you have many, many traits that set you up to be effective as a leader, but we all have some that don't play well into leadership.

In working with hundreds of school leaders, here are some of the hardest traits I've found to work around in order to be effective:

- Perfectionism;
- People-pleasing;
- Procrastination.

Chances are you're like, hey! I'm all of those at one time or another! That's probably the norm. Being a *little* of any of these won't derail your leadership. Being *overly obsessed* with any of these can cause a school leader great difficulty.

Perfectionism. Plainly stated, *school administration is really hard for perfectionists.* Doesn't mean that they can't do it, but without some modifications, your road may be one full of ongoing stress. If you have a job that is more specific, more discrete in what you do, you may be able to use your perfectionism to your advantage.

Understanding the difference between healthy striving and perfectionism is critical to laying down the shield and picking up your life. Research shows that perfectionism hampers success. In fact, it's often the path to depression, anxiety, addiction, and life paralysis.
~Brene Brown

When you're in school administration, you will not always get it right. You won't always win. Sometimes things will happen that will cause you heartburn that you could not have prevented no matter what you did. Since you're in charge, you are accountable for what happens at your school, but you're not *responsible* for everything that takes place. So, you get the blame when someone
74

else has messed up. This doesn't always sit well with perfectionists.

Even moreso, when school is done properly, it's a place of learning. Learning is a *progress-based* endeavor, and not a perfectionist one. Things get messy at a school; the most effective leader guides the school through the rapids, not avoids them.

How does the perfectionist make it in school administration? You learn to adapt. YES you plan, but you plan so you'll be comfortable in your adjustments as they are required. Things that seem very big at the moment aren't always so when given the benefit of time and perspective. Training yourself to see the bigger picture can help you maintain your standards of performance without being as vulnerable to the stress of leading in an environment that is fraught with imperfections. Loving those around you for their progress while keeping a vision of their excellence can help keep things moving forward to that better place.

People-pleasing. Most people would prefer that others like them. It's when you *sacrifice other priorities and values* to avoid conflict and to please others that it becomes a problem.As the leader, if your priority is to be liked, you are likely to make many bad decisions.

Granted, it's not a good strategy to see how many people you can get to *dislike* you either! The answer lives in the vision and purpose of your school. If you build that vision *collectively* with your people AND you review it annually to adapt and maintain clarity, then when you make decisions appropriate to the vision and mission, you ARE pleasing people by being a *guardian of the school's values.*

A focus on vision, mission, purpose and values keeps your focus away from personal preferences, promises, favors and drama. If you can get this part right, you are exempt from reading the rest of this book! This ONE thing alone will set you up for all the success you can handle. (Please keep reading anyway, though.)

<u>Procrastination.</u>   It is acceptable (even advisable) to take a moment to make decisions and not be rushed into judgment before you have gathered all of the information needed to make that decision right. That's not procrastination… that's good leadership.

It's procrastination *when you have a problem that will be uncomfortable to address and your plan is to hope it gets better on its own.* For example, if you have a teacher who isn't performing up to the school's standards, you should develop a strategy and get busy with it. When you are new to a school, the people around you already know who is doing what they're supposed to do and who isn't. They'll give you a brief grace period for you to figure it out, and after that they expect you'll address it.

Doing what needs to be done may not make you happy, but it will make you great.

~George Bernard Shaw

If you don't address the poor behaviors among faculty and staff, the people who do what they're supposed to do will begin to ask themselves, "well why does it matter?" You are reliant on a high percentage of people doing what they're supposed to do… if you have those who don't (or won't) the others are watching to see what you'll do. After a period of time, they begin to think it's no longer a teacher problem…but now an administrator problem.

FINITE RESOURCES

Time is more valuable than money.
You can get more money but
you cannot get more time.

~Jim Rohn

Time, Money, and Energy.

Three finite resources. How you choose to allocate them reveals what you value and determines what you accomplish.

Finite Resources
1. Time
2. Money
3. Energy/Enthusiasm

I've heard it said that if you want to know what someone values, check out their calendar and their checkbook. One can *say* they value a lot of things, but we tend to put our money and our time where our priority is. When you become the principal, *your choices of where you spend your time and where you put your energy reveal to everyone what's important to you.* Remember, they don't always read what you write or hear what you say, but they almost always see what you do.

Time. You have the same amount of time as everyone else. Not any more, not any less. Now, as principal, you have more things to do than most anyone else, so something has to give. The archetype for principal has been to let everything else go in a swap to get things done. That's an option, but one with some severe tradeoffs.

Remember that every choice you make to do something is simultaneously a choice to *NOT* do something else. You choose to stay late and get some data tidied up… you choose not to go to the gym that day. You choose to take a lot of work home… you choose not to engage with the people you live with when you get there.

Nearly every school principal I have worked with laments the issue of time… until they realize that it's a fixed quantity and that *no matter how smart you are and how hard you work, you can't. Do. It. All.*

While you're struggling with time, you're really waiting until you can acquiesce to the nature of your job… that you have more to do than you can do and that you become better when you learn to prioritize and select the most high-impact uses of your time. When people ask me for help in time management, I work quickly to show them that its really *priority management.*

I know what you're thinking… These things *still* have to be done. You're right. That's why there are additional choices to *Do* or *Not Do.* (shoutout to Yoda) You can also choose to *Direct* things, and even better, you can choose to *Delegate* them. It's really probably better stated that you *Empower*, but you know us educators are obsessed with alliteration, so let me have Delegate if you would, please.

Nearly every school principal I have worked with laments the issue of time... until they realize that it's a fixed quantity and that no matter how smart you are and how hard you work, you can't. Do. It. All.

Placed in front of you thousands of times every day are potential actions with which you choose one of the four... Do, Direct, Delegate, Don't Do. As you grow as a leader you begin to refine your processes to get more done by using the range of all four.

You do things that *only* the principal can do. You direct things that don't need your total involvement but aren't ready to be completely handed off. You delegate *ANYTHING* you can delegate. The rule of thumb for a principal is *if someone else can do it, you should empower them to do so.* (Because the list of things that only the principal can do is massive and you won't be able to do everything that's just on that list!)

Finally, deciding what *NOT* to do is the hidden piece of leadership you learn through experience. I know you've been sold on the merits of *servant leadership.* It's important that your people see you as one of them... not afraid to get your hands dirty... not looking at things as beneath you to do.

That *doesn't* mean that you do everything, everywhere, all at once. (shoutout to Michelle Yeoh) Your willingness to do anything shouldn't be misconstrued as additional job duties. Sure, you should roll up your sleeves on a big task and get in there with the others for the esprit de corps but it has to be situational. The principal's work is the day-to-day confirming and reshaping of norms… the clarifying of the vision…leading others to be as effective as possible. You do this via many avenues… inspiration, motivation, feedback, evaluation, modeling. It takes tens of thousands of conversations to bring the actions of your people to work in harmony. So, it's all right to mop when someone drops their coffee, but you shouldn't do it all day.

Money. In schools, we transfer "money" into human resources and those resources into serving children or supporting those who do. It's finite and the truth is *never enough for the increasingly intricate goals we have assumed in schools.* When we discuss money for the school administrator, other than supplies, grants, and special ear-marks, the bulk of your funding goes to personnel (usually around 90% or more).

So what does that mean for the school-level administrator?

For you to be a good steward of the finite resource of money that you've been allotted, *you want to maximize your capacity to engage your people in meaningful, effective work.* As the leader of the school, one of your main jobs is to work with real, live humans so everything you do requires differentiation.

Something I've noted among school administrators is the tendency to view our people two-dimensionally. We often look at our people as being fixed in a particular way. That has not been my experience with humans. It's like we aren't working on land, but in a river. Even if we are in the same place in the river, *every day is a different experience.* The water is different, often due to factors outside of our control. We have to adapt to what we find around us and how it is ever changing.

So when we make caricatures out of our faculty and staff in our minds (good teachers, bad teachers, etc…) we do so without acknowledging the *constantly changing conditions* around our people. The context of their lives away from school… their relationships with colleagues… their personal health. They aren't the same every day, every year for thirty years!

As the leader, that should bring you some hope. People can grow. But as the leader, you should be a part of that growth in your work with them. Remember the employees you have who are doing it like you love it aren't guaranteed to do that again tomorrow. Remember to notice not just when people do poorly, but even more so when they do right. When the boss acknowledges it, they are likely to repeat it.

Energy. Of the big three resources that the school administrator juggles, this is the one that I think is the key. Mainly because the other two have mechanisms to monitor and moderate them. THIS one depends on you to handle on your own and that's not always as easy as just saying it.

For time, you have a calendar. For money, you have a budget and an allotment sheet. For energy? You have crashing and getting sick. Maybe we can do better than that.

As the leader, you already know that you'll run out of time before you run out of tasks. I have found that you'll run out of energy before you run out of time, if not now, before you know it.

Ever get home and just collapse in the chair? Pajamas on by 7:30 on a Friday night? Ever tell the people you live with that you are not currently fielding questions, making decisions, or solving conflicts?

You are a school administrator!

Nearly every task and action you engage in as a school administrator requires large quantities of energy. Ever work on bringing about a change at your school? THAT takes extra energy. When you're working on change, you are facing a force that pushes back on you called *BWADITW*, which is slightly stronger than gravity.

BWADITW (But we've always done it this way) requires large amounts of energy from you, a reason that you don't want to bring about too much change all at once. There are many reasons but one big one is that *you'll run out of energy* and *BWADITW* will roll over you like that rock in Raiders of the Lost Ark (shoutout to Harrison Ford).

It's not only large change initiatives that require a large investment of your energy. It's a one-on-one conversation with a teacher. It's an IEP meeting that lasts three hours. It's supervising activities for hours after you've already worked 9-10 hours during the day.

Managing your energy is critical, so please remember this: you need to get adequate rest. You need to disengage your brain from thinking about school all the time. You need a hobby. You will be better when you allow yourself time for rest and recovery.

And, there are people who suck every bit of energy from you (shoutout to Jon Gordon) and there are those who multiply any energy you expend with them right back at you. THOSE are the people you should choose to spend time with. It's easier to lift a school up from the top… it's too heavy to push up from the bottom. Intentionally spend time with those who will lift you up. You'll be a better leader for it.

JUDGMENT

*Good judgement comes
from experience and
often experience
comes from bad judgment.*

~Rita Mae Brown

When you're the principal, everyone is watching you. They listen to what you say, watch what you do, see what must be your priorities (by what you spend the most time doing) and they pay attention to decisions you make.

As the leader of the school, you make hundreds of decisions a day. Your judgment is a matter of interest to the others at the school (teachers, staff, parents, students) depending on how much it relates to them. If you begin to write a letter of concern whenever any of your teachers are tardy to school, the decision to do so will be of interest to all of your teachers, not just the tardy ones, because it has the potential to affect them.

If you decide that you will no longer allow check outs at your school after lunch, your judgment will be measured by parents, staff, and others.

If you make a decision regarding consequences for a violation of the student code of conduct that others feel is too easy/too hard, your judgment will come into consideration.

You're in charge. You can't make everyone happy. Should you really worry about whether people are happy with the decisions you make?

It's not about making people happy with your decisions, but it IS about people having confidence in your decision-making processes and ultimately your judgment. Judgment is one of the "Big Three" things that everyone around you is using to assess you as the leader. They observe your **judgment,** your **results**, and your **treatment of others.** In summary, people are assessing your worth as the leader based on *what you do, the manner in which you do it, and whether it works.*

Here's a pathway to better judgment:

1.) <u>Have a process for making decisions.</u> Most of the "bad judgment" episodes that I encounter in the field are principals who didn't go through a thorough process of arriving at their decision. Your process should include a series of questions intended to distill the situation in a logical manner.

2.) <u>Avoid haste; avoid emotion.</u> Almost all of the instances I've seen with principals regarding the use of bad judgment involve a lack of patience and/or an abundance of emotion. Neither serve you well when making decisions.

3.) <u>Listen and learn from other sources.</u> If you make your mind up and then seek others to go along with you, this isn't a decision-making process, but it's a consensus-building event. They have their place in leadership, but if you truly are seeking assistance in decision making, listen objectively to trusted sources, gain missing data, and be as exhaustive in your search as you're able given the context of being principal.

After going through your process, you'll make a decision that may not please everyone, but you will gain their confidence by listening, having a process, and sharing (as is applicable given the circumstance) *<u>why</u>* you've made the decision you've made.

HABITS

*In a nutshell, your
health, wealth, happiness,
fitness and success
depend on your habits.*

~Joanna Jast

You want to do well as a principal, so you expend a lot of your energy to do so. You fret about burning up all of your time and energy before you make it home to spend time with the ones who love you most.

Balance is often on your mind if you're a principal, and most of the time the questions I get from our colleagues on the subject are asked in great hopes that I can share the secret to getting in balance.

*This is as close as you'll get to a "secret"
on balance, so, listen up, please.*

To get yourself closer to balanced, you need to not only be full of enthusiasm and energy at school. You also need to bring it at home. That's a problem since we do school for most of the day and inevitably are more tired by the time we return home than when we arrive at school.

So, you need more energy! The secret there? Being more healthy. There are traps all around you for that! How do you get there?

Habits.

Habits are either working for you or against you. If you want to be more balanced, you have to have more energy, which is more likely if you're healthier. To be healthier is all about habits.

Habits have often been a struggle for me, so I have learned a lot to share with you, not necessarily by getting this right but by learning from experience.

Healthy habits are about sleep, exercise, and what we eat. As a principal, you basically live in a minefield of bad habits all around you. It's easy to get into negative habits that will eat away at your energy in the short run and at your overall health and wellness in the long run.

It seemed like it was all good for me while I was principal. Went to bed late, got to school early, went at my job with lots of energy and enthusiasm every morning! Around 10:00 AM, it was time for my treat for having gotten off to a good start. It's number: 61. It's name: The Big Texas Cinnamon Roll. The recipe: Seven seconds in the microwave, washed down with a Diet Coke. It was like Christmas morning every day, only a few steps from the main office.

The bad part of that story isn't even the cinnamon roll; it's the every day part. It's SO easy to get into habits that lead to negative results. After fighting through a period of tiredness around 4:00 PM, I'd have

a little time to work before going to a school activity. There was always food to purchase at the ball games. The convenience was addictive. It was also taking away my energy by the end of the work day.

It's really because of the busy-ness of the job that many of our decisions turn into negative habits. You make poor food choices because it's convenient. You stay up too late because you want to get work done, but also because you're tired and it takes longer. You really really really are going to walk/run/go to the gym tomorrow. Really.

Despite all of the challenges about poor habits and principals, there is hope. Lots of it!

It's called **today.** The best, healthiest, most energy-producing habit you'll ever have began by doing it once. As they say on the Lottery commercials, *today could be the day!* Unlike the lottery, your chances of success are much greater. It's a decision, and you are good with those.

Balance is more likely with more energy, and energy is directly related to healthy habits. Don't worry about how you'll get it right six weeks from now. Don't regret how you didn't get it right yesterday. Today. Habits. Success. You can do it!

CRITICISM

*If you want to make everyone happy,
don't be a leader; sell ice cream.*

~attributed to Steve Jobs

How do you handle criticism? Does it bother you when people talk about you? If you administer an anonymous survey and you get negative feedback do you spend time thinking about who said what? When your judgment is called into question, how quickly are you able to move forward from the criticism and into the work?

One of the most challenging things for many school administrators is the **volume of criticism** that is directed at you when you're in a position of leadership. You can't let the criticism that comes with the job paralyze you from doing it effectively. The same is true with praise; it's no more effective to **cling only to praise** and put blinders on to valuable feedback and critical needs.

As it so often seems with leadership, the answer **lies in the space between.** Neither sidetracked nor oblivious to things others say.

In many ways, being a **principal** is a LOT more like being a classroom teacher than being an assistant principal. In both of those roles, you **lead a group of people on a journey to success.** You bring them together as a team. You differentiate what you do to meet the needs of the different members of the team. You encourage. You inspire. You direct, and you show them a vision of what 'good' looks like. *When they want to join you,* they become part of the team.

Remember that you've done this before, many times. With children and/or adolescents. What's different now is that you're working with adults (!), your "classroom" is much bigger, and **lots more people are able to see what you do and how you do it.** Beyond that, there are a lot of similarities from classroom teaching.

There are always (at least when people have been normally distributed) some members of your team who are **enthusiastic,** while others are in some form or fashion **visibly against** whatever journey this is you've invited them to join.

And, like your classroom and your school there are others who are very critical... those who are lost in what's happening, those who are waiting to see how it goes, and those who want to read the details before they commit to the whole trek.

WHILE you're leading, you will be criticized for your choices... for going one way instead of another. For not giving enough notice. You'll also be praised by the enthusiasts for your bravery in leading the way. Either of those voices can keep you from getting the team where it needs to go. You should hunt for something more.

When a group is normally distributed, there are about the same percentage of people who are super-positive and are enthusiasts as there are those who are against change, growth, and the people who bring it. (In schools it actually seems to skew to the positive, so you most likely have more positives than negatives.). And while these members of your team are certainly important and valuable to the journey, a team with ONLY them will struggle toward success. You need people around you to encourage you, but not when you're about to make bad decisions that lead the group away from the goal. You need encouragers, but don't wish that everyone were them; healthy teams value TRUST at a higher level than fear of conflict. (from Patrick Lencioni's Five Dysfunctions of a Team) Don't wallow in criticism, but don't overdose on praise either.

SO if you don't get taken over by the criticism nor the praise, what are you then focused on? **The Vision**. In leading change you can move forward effectively once you gather a critical mass. You can't do that only with the enthusiasts, and it's a hard push with the objectors. There are others though that are available and to engage them you need to clarify the vision.

When you're leading the journey to success, you'll always have some watchers who sit in the back to see how it's going to go. They aren't against this effort, but they aren't quite confident that it's going to work for them to move too quickly. There are others in your expedition that are genuinely lost. Maybe they're new and inexperienced. Maybe they're busy. Regardless, they're not with you yet and not against you, but they need some direction.

People process things differently. People on your team (in your school) don't process in the same manner that you do. It doesn't make them bad, or uncooperative, or anything. It means they don't do it like you do.

Remember, you've done this before. You will ALWAYS have people who need more information, have to put it in their terms, do additional research or consternation. Give them space to breathe and the information they need. LISTEN to them more than tell, as this is their process to come to understanding. Work to make it easy for others to ask questions. There's an oft-used phrase in school administration that makes me cringe. It's "don't bring me a problem without bringing a solution." If that's your culture it's your choice, but you are cutting off people who need to say it out loud, and you also are shunning those who are good at identifying problems (which is a really important skill for any team).

Part III. Reaching Out

PEOPLE WORK

If you do not treat people with the respect they deserve, do not expect any kind of commitment to your productivity goals and target.
~Ian Fuhr

If you were somehow able to work all day and all night, seven days a week, you *still* wouldn't be "caught up" in the work of a principal. There are always emails to reply to, spreadsheets to study, paperwork to get done.

That's what gets a lot of new principals… they place a very high value on this elusive thing of *being caught up* and they miss out on prioritizing things that are of a higher value. I know that many of you come into the job taking pride in getting things done, getting tasks completed, checking things off of your list.

But what if your check list doesn't have the most highly-valuable actions on it?

School is simple, but it's not easy. From a management point of view, teachers are the key to success at school. One of my superintendents, Stan DeJarnett, frequently said that there were two kinds of people who worked in our system: teachers, and people who supported teachers.

No doubt that many of the things that you do as a school administrator are done in the name of supporting teachers. If you don't get your Title I budget submitted, you're going to be short on funds that are tied to staffing. Spending time addressing student behavior is important to your teachers, and explicitly viewed as

92

support by them. Attending IEP meetings and PLCs are definitely teacher support.

All of those things are good things to do. You could stay busy all the time doing things that no one would argue against you doing. The challenge is to plan to do the things that are **most** critical for the work of your school every week and every day.

You have to determine what those things are within the context of where you're working and the moment in time you're working there. Your system may have expressed some points of emphasis; you may have data that suggest particular areas of need.

During the school year, most systems have teachers at work for 7 ½ hours over 190 days. That's the total time you have to work with. Much of that time is available for you to observe, assess, and create diagnostic plans for your teachers. Much *less* of that time is available for you to engage in conversation with your teachers.

This is one of the fundamental design flaws of our profession. Your success depends upon successfully teaching *what we do and how we do it* to your teachers. The time period you have to do so is extremely limited. Let's assume you are working at a middle school and you have 90 minutes of planning time (professional time might be a better name) for each of your teachers. Those ninety minutes are all-inclusive from bell-to-bell. If your teachers are guiding students on and off the hallway for connections, we have to deduct that time, as well as time for a convenience break. We're now at 75 minutes, but you can't have that available for your usage every day because they have PLCs, SSTs, IEPs, 504s, and other meetings that will take some of that time. On some days you can get to anyone, others you can get to no one.

Let's say you have two four-member teams, plus student services teachers, so each of your grade levels has ten teachers that you want to get to. And, let's ambitiously shoot for three days each week in which teachers are available for you to coach or plan individually or in a group setting. Out of the three days they are available, you are only able to get there for two of them because of principal meetings, training, issues at the school requiring the principal (big behavior incidents, etc…) So now we're down to two days a week, 36 weeks of the school year.

Over the course of a school year that gives you this, per grade-level:

- 72 potential slots of 75 minutes each
- Ten teachers
- Ten preplanning, professional development, and postplanning days. (Teacher availability to the principal varies between school systems)

If you split up the time evenly for 1:1 conversations, you'll have **seven segments** of 75 minutes with each teacher throughout the year. Perhaps you'll choose to meet with some of the teachers in pairs? Maybe as teams? What do your teachers need?

As we move through a period of a limited supply of interested teachers (more limited in some areas than others), it's likely that your teachers will need *more* of your time instead of less. And, yes, you can engage instructional coaches and assistant principals to be a part of these conversations but it's likely they have a full schedule as well.

Here's the math of it all: while you are there at school when the teachers and students are there, you would be well-served in spending your time on peoplework rather than paperwork. You have such limited availability to get to them that you should take it when it comes.

And, it would be advantageous for you to develop strategies on delivering that peoplework. Setting a schedule at the beginning of the year would help keep you on track. Having areas of emphasis that you focus on across the board (differentiated for the needs of the teachers) can help you target a focus and give you a scope for your work.

Many principals look at the limited time and choose to spend it with the most at-risk teachers they have. Some of it is survival– some of our newer teachers may need our most intense support to make it.

The problem with that approach is in leaving your top teachers without improvement and without validation. Think of them as being your Tier I teachers. They are able to meet the expected level of competency at your school with only the support that everyone gets. (It's not a rating system, the same as with our students; only a tiered approach of how much support someone needs to be successful).

If you spend all of your time with your Tier II and Tier III teachers, you run the risk that your Tier I teachers might not stay there. Just like with students, Tier I members can become Tier II when they aren't recognized for what they're doing. For the most part your Tier I teachers *want* to do a good job and want to please the principal, especially at the elementary levels. If you fail to recognize and acknowledge the good things they are doing, *they may quit doing them* either in search of what you *are* looking for or in frustration that their efforts aren't being noticed.

At the core of what your job is this layer of motivation and inspiration. Your words, your time, your attention play into how your teachers feel about school and have an influence on how much they commit to their job, and how well they do it. Making a commitment to the *peoplework* leads to success.

COMMUNICATION

The art of communication is the language of leadership.

~James Humes

What's your job when you're the principal? Vision, expectations, focus, and communication. The first three of these depend greatly on your ability to do the last. And, if you ask people who work in a school what needs to be improved upon, the Family Feud number one answer is most likely going to be… Communication! (With "discipline" and "morale" likely in the top five as well)

Why is communication such a regular concern at a school? Well, because we are part of the school, it's harder to see, but if you back up and get a broader perspective, it's easy to see why effective communication is always a premium in schools.

First off, the volume of things to be communicated is massive. What to do, when to do it; how we'd like it done. Student information systems, reading programs, and emergency procedures; attendance, grading, and parental contacts. There are SO MANY moving parts in any school that communication is a challenge from the sheer volume of information that needs to be shared.

And for all of that information, we have precious little time in which to share it. Think about it. Other occupations have time set aside for sharing ideas, clarifying understandings, and answering questions. Our primary, frontline workforce -- our teachers -- have supervisory duties for nearly the entirety of their work day. Teachers and school leaders aren't (or shouldn't be) available all day to read and reply to emails. There are very narrow windows of time that information can be exposed to the people who need it.

Finally, a lot of school communication is compliance driven rather than effectiveness-minded. The object of communication isn't in telling, but is for the other person to understand and be able to move forward with that information. As the principal, it's not enough for you to say, "but I told them!" Your value as a leader (intentionally saying this several times in the book in case you noticed...) is measured by what others do. *"But I told them "* doesn't serve as an explanation or excuse if your people don't accomplish what was needed or requested. It's up to you to figure out how to effectively communicate with your people. Tell them again... tell them a different way... get them to tell the instructions back to you in their understanding. Communication is rarely a one-and-done thing. Think of it like you do tiered instruction; you hope that your "Tier I" communication successfully connects with a high percentage of your people (80% is really good based on normal distribution). Then, you go into other ways to meet the communication needs of your Tier II and Tier III teachers.

If you're thinking, yeah, that's cool, but I barely have time for the Tier I communication... I get it, but here's the thing: communication IS your job. (Or at least a very big part of it) You want to learn from your people and learn what works to activate information into performance. Again, your work isn't in the telling, but in *their* understanding AND application.

Effective communication is four-part harmony.

1. The Sender;
2. The Message;
3. The Method;
4. The Receiver.

For communication to lead to action, it needs to hit all four parts. As the sender, you are most effective when you can bring focus and clarity to the idea that you want to share. The message itself is key; if you're sending an email, remember to stop typing before your recipients stop reading (which is typically measured by the "no-scroll" rule. If you have to scroll down to read the email, *most of your recipients aren't going to read it.*

Think about your messaging like packing for a long trip; lay out everything you're thinking about taking and then put half of it back up. Same for emails and other communication. Do you edit your emails? You should. *But I don't have time...* well, remember your goal... influence actions through effective communication. Take the time to condense your message and say it in fewer words.

The method in which we send out messages is also something worthy of your consideration. During the 2020-2021 school year, everyone learned how to screencast. That's an effective method of communication as you can share your ideas and your face/voice (allowing space for tone and inflection) in a format that your people can choose to watch at a convenient time for them. That would be a method you may want to consider continuing to use for communication post-blip. A pro-tip is to keep it at five minutes or less.

Another method of communication that you may want to consider is expanding the screencast concept to develop a library of staff-only videos that are your "How To…" do things at your school. For example, when schools begin the year with the bookkeeper explaining how field trips are to be done, that is an example of poorly-planned communication. It's done "in-case" and not "in-time". If you ask your bookkeeper to make that same presentation via video and include it in your library of "How To…" videos for your school, now when that teacher gets ready to plan a field trip in February, the information is available for when she needs it.

Think about that method and how you can use it to communicate not only logistical items but deeper ones as well. Why not ask one of your all-star teachers to make a 4-5 minute video on "How I Connect With Students" that you put in your video library? You and your administrative team can use it as a professional learning tool to support your classroom observations, and teachers can use it when they choose to as well. There are infinite possibilities for communicating effectively by asking your *teachers and staff* to share practices, procedures and protocols in this way.

Finally, effective communication depends upon the recipient. If someone was walking past you with their hands full and boxes stacked so high that they had to look around them to see where they were going, would you ask that person to carry something else at that time? Well, no. Same thing with communication. If you *really* want to effectively communicate, you meet the recipient where and when they are. Using screencasts can be a help in allowing your recipient to pick a moment that works to hear what you're saying. A really good book to help you understand the teachable/learnable moment is *When*, by Daniel Pink. In it, he shares the science behind the timing of our actions and suggests that not only is "timing everything" as we've always heard, but *everything is timing*. When you communicate can be as critical to effectiveness as *what* you communicate. (Note: Best time to ask for permission/blessing/favors from your supervisor is Tuesday morning around 9:00 AM, according to Pink)

By The Way, Don't Just Distribute Information

According to researcher and author Phillip Jackson in his book, *Life in Classrooms,*

"elementary school teachers average 200-300 exchanges with students each hour accumulating between 1200-1500 unplanned and unpredictable exchanges that require teacher decisions and judgements. That, is exhausting."

Larry Cuban compares teaching to being a jazz musician or a basketball player. These are worlds of improvisation, guided by concepts, but reliant on the artist for success. Wynston Marsalis is epic at the trumpet and Lebron James is equally artistic with the basketball. Both of them seem to be tireless in their pursuit of excellence, but yet they don't approach the volume of work that our teachers are doing every day, everywhere. They build in rehearsal, rest and recovery into their performance. Our teachers? We ask them to do lesson-planning and calls home on their time off.

It is actually amazing that we accomplish what we do with what we are asking of our teachers (and their administrators too!). Remember the volume of energy-draining exchanges and micro-decisioning that your teachers are doing all day the next time you want to give them some information at the end of the school day. (Note: 2:55 PM is the lowest time for energy and learning for most people according to Pink in *When*, so launching big ideas then is... not the best strategy.)

So your success depends upon your teachers' performance, you have tons of things that you'd like to/need to share with them and there's hardly any time, and the time you have isn't prime time.

Next job metaphor: be a funnel.

Not *that kind* of funnel. Think about the funnel that helps you put gasoline in your lawnmower. Wide at the top. Very narrow at the bottom. Controlling what's distributed so it doesn't pour out everywhere.

Teachers don't need you to forward everything to them. They don't need the long version. They need the executive summary. Try getting feedback from a teacher or two before you send something to everybody. (Share the wealth and ask different people each time so you get different perspectives)

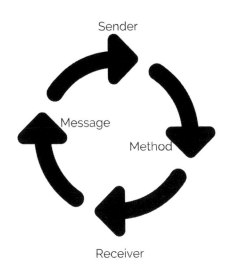

If you *really* want your communication to be effective, it's going to take a lot of work. This is such a critical part of your success as the principal, yet it seems to be undervalued as we often expect that just because we send it that it lands where we want it to go. Work on the four-parts of communication and watch the positive effects it has on morale and on performance.

LISTENING

Be as passionate about listening as you are about wanting to be heard.

~Brene Brown

You are incredibly busy when you're a school administrator. And, you realize that your success is *directly related to what and how the people in your school do their jobs.* So it's easy to fall into a habit of *constantly telling people things.* You have SO much to say (Shoutout Dave Matthews) and so little time in which to say it that you can feel rushed, urgent, even panicked to get it all out.

Slow down.

Telling isn't teaching. Monologue isn't communication.

Listen.

Whatever you want to share makes sense to you in your head, but if it doesn't connect with your intended target, it was all a waste of time. How do you manicure your message to get it through?

Listen.

You need to understand where the other person is before you pour your knowledge, expertise, and instructions on them. The absence of effective communication slows down progress. Saying it doesn't always get the job done. You need to slow down and listen.

What I've come to believe is that while listening is a skill, it's just as much an *attitude.* If you approach communicating with others as a checklist ("check! I told Ms. Williams about reading groups.) then you can proudly mark off that you complied and told them. If you are interested in their effective use of what you shared, think about them as you did one of your students when you were in the classroom. You don't just say it once... you say it, they say it, they do it, you talk about it. Teach, don't tell.

Remember that at ALL times you are not only working on performance but also ATTITUDES about performance. When you communicate information with others, HOW you do so is as important as the message itself. How you act when you deliver information to others has an impact on how they receive it. If you act frustrated as you deliver information, your teachers are going to feel that and it's going to change the recipe. The attitude of a listener is described in the five points here:

1. Listens to Understand: When you are the leader, everyone wants a minute of your time. The most effective leaders *really* listen to others (rather than formulate your response while they're talking). More than that, you go beyond the question or concern to the reason behind it. When you listen to understand, you are interacting with your people; when you listen to *reply* you are merely responding to them. It's the subtleties that make the difference between struggling and successful leaders.

2. Values and Respects Others: You may have 150 conversations during the course of work hours but to those who speak with you, it might be their most important conversation of the day. Their time with you might be the subject of dinner conversation at home or the first thing they share with their significant other. The most effective leader embraces the role and makes interactions with faculty, staff, students, and parents important. This is an inside-out action; you have to first value and respect others in a genuine way to be able to communicate with them as such. They will know from your tone, your level of attention, and how you speak with them. And, if they believe you value and respect them they will be more likely to join you on your school's journey to success.

3. Speaks Well, Not Ill of Others: Speaking negatively of others is an invitation for your team to do the same. If you, however, are caught speaking well about other people, it shows that you notice and that you care.

4. Communicates Clearly and Concisely: The leader can often have the burden of knowing too much. All of the things that we are asked to initiate at our schools are complicated and voluminous. We do well when we filter all of the things we know into bite-size portions that our teachers can swallow. The most effective leaders also proofread and have others read their work for clarity. It ALWAYS makes sense in your head; will it make the same sense in someone else's?

5. Shares Information in a Timely and Appropriate Manner: Teachers don't like surprises unless they are chocolate covered. Keep information flowing in a timely way. When we get information distributed timely and effectively, it helps our team grow confidence in our leadership. When we are getting important things out at the last minute all the time, our teachers begin to wonder about our ability to steer the ship. Little things get to be big things.

YOUR PHONE

*89% of Americans check their phones
within ten minutes of waking up.*

*The average American checks
their phone 144 times a day.*

*~Survey by Reviews.org
2023*

Imagine that you're a principal and you've joined your colleagues for the leadership meeting with the superintendent and staff at the central office. **The year is 2002.** It's five years before the birth of the first iPhone (June 29, 2007) and another year before the Blackberry RIM 850 and 857 debut.

Now, for a moment, imagine that you have brought with you to the meeting your mail. I'm not talking about your laptop or tablet (we didn't even have tablets); there's not much in the way of wifi so that's not it. Imagine instead that you have brought your U.S. Postal Service-delivered, sealed in envelopes, stamped and processed, actual mail. Maybe for fun you have a really big rubber band around it to keep it together. See the picture?

There you are at the meeting: you, your fellow principals, the superintendent's staff, the superintendent, and... your stack of mail. With the big red (or green) rubber band.

The meeting begins well enough, but as time goes on, you sort of get a little disinterested. The topics aren't items that are really specific to you and your school and, well, you have this stack of mail to look at. So, you pull out your letter opener, make an incision, and open up a piece of mail. You read it over, glancing back up at the meeting and its attendees every so often. Just for effect, you even nod occasionally at something that someone else says even though you really aren't sure what they said, but you do look like you're paying attention anyway.

Can you imagine that scene? Well of course not! You would have been stared down by your colleagues first, then by the directors, and if you didn't stop looking at your mail soon enough, the superintendent would have most likely addressed your behavior. This would not have been acceptable.

Why then, do so many principals, assistant principals, and other school leaders look at their phones when they're around other people? Have our jobs become that hypersensitive? Are things **that** tenuous that we have to be at that level of alert at all times? Most likely not.

Do we even *intend* to look at our phones all the time? I don't think so, and neither does Larry Rosen, author and psychologist who suggests that our incessant viewing of our phones is potentially: addiction; obsession, a social shield.

For the leader, any of those root causes of this behavior can be detrimental to our ability to lead our schools and the people in them. Here's a challenge for you:

- Pick a day to get a baseline;
- How often do you check your phone between the time you get to work and when the school day proper concludes? (buses, students and teachers have departed) Count your glances; record them (where else? in the notes section of your phone), and then begin to see where you are.

If you are looking at your phone more frequently than you are seeking out others to have face-to-face engagement, you may have an issue that will need addressing.

DIALOGUE

Dialogue is a non-confrontational communication, where both parties are willing to learn from each other and therefore leads much farther into finding new grounds together.

~Scilla Elworthy

Recently, I was with one of the wonderful principals that I support who had a question. She had observed a class that had left her... underwhelmed. The teacher had not really created the engaging classroom of curiosity, innovation, and learning that the principal was seeking. It was a relatively low level... most of the work done by the teacher, peripheral topics, low student engagement. The sort of thing that once was commonplace but is no longer our standard for excellence anywhere.

The principal's question was this: **what do you say in conversation with the teacher to improve instruction?** It's a fundamental question and one that everyone who observes classes should consider. Remember, all of our efforts in teacher evaluation should be for the purpose of improving instruction. That means that completing the observation is only a step in the process. It's like putting a coat of primer on a wall. It's just not finished!

Observations are important... if they lead to improving instruction. The road between the two is the conversation between administrator and teacher. That critical portion of the process requires the proper mindset in order to be successful.

In short it's this: the most important part of the post-observation conference isn't what you as the administrator say. **The most**

important part is the teacher's understanding of what should be done to improve instruction. It's not just semantics; it's a very real thing. As an administrator, the critical task of such a conference is to be **useful.** Not brilliant, not clever, not annoyingly comprehensive, but... useful.

It's really about developing a dialogue rather than a download.

A download is when you drop all the knowledge you've prepared on the teacher, or if you will permit, *the intended target.* We usually do this as administrators in what we believe to be a creative manner. We'll begin the meeting by asking our teacher, "so, how do you think it went?" While questions are the gateway to understanding, that particular one is a relatively meager one to ask. There are many other questions to ask, but that one is usually followed by... the download. This happens quite frequently: the administrator asks, "how do you think it went?", followed by the teacher sharing her version and then, here it comes! The administrator "goes over" her observations. The meeting concludes with a ranking of some sort, which either ends with satisfaction on the part of the teacher, or dissatisfaction which leads to some defensive statements, maybe a few suggestions, but not *really* what the process was intended to be.

Instead of the download, you need a dialogue, and here's the main reason why. The teacher has to process what happened and figure out:

- That there's a discrepancy between what happened in the classroom and what *ought* to happen in the classroom;
- That there are steps she can take to lead a more improved classroom the next time they gather.

This IS the key part, and quite often it's missed. Unless the teacher sorts it out in her head and can truly see her classroom for what it is (and what it isn't) any actions taken will be in the name of compliance. Her attempt to satisfy the conclusions you've reached at the end of your observation download. That's not progress; that's just a game of cat and mouse.

INSTEAD, the most effective administrators are skillful in **leading others into a dialogue.** You ask questions; you create scenarios; you ask your teacher to paint a picture of what it ought to look like; you don't just download. You talk. But you do more than that. You lead your teacher to a deeper understanding of what her classroom ought to be. You do so in a manner in which she can relate. There's not one script for this to follow; instead, it's a differentiated approach designed to relate to the way the teacher you're conferencing with processes and understands.

And at the end of such a conference, there's a different kind of feeling. A feeling that you are there to be useful in helping your teacher grow. Not an argument over whether something occurred, whether it usually occurs, or anything like that. If you invest the time into having quality conferences, you will be on the path to supporting your teachers in their journey to success, and that's a place you'll be welcomed.

TECH IS A TOOL

... manage your phone. Don't let it manage you.

~Sir Richard Branson

Don't let your technology run your life. Here's what happens to many new principals. You want to make a good first impression. (Smart) You want to be approachable. (Yes!) So you become obsessed with how quickly you can respond to everyone who emails, calls, or messages you. That is good... to a point.

All of the good will that you garner by being uber-available and super-quick to reply goes down the drain when you are face-to-face with one of your people and you feel that tingle and... you lift your arm up to see what message your Apple watch is bringing you.

It's great to have access to modes of communication; it's even more important to be **present.**

You will want to know what the system's expectations are about responding to messages and emails. It's important to comply with the established protocols.

Beyond that, you should establish and communicate *your protocols with your people.* For example, you may want to tell your faculty and staff that regular text messages and emails are reserved for a certain time period (6:00 AM- 8:00 PM?) on school days. You pick the time that works for you and make sure that you too follow it.

One of the most harmful things that can happen to you in school administration is if you go into Waffle House mode. Always open. It only works for them because they have multiple shifts. For you, it is a recipe for exhaustion. Your brain needs breaks and if you are constantly plugged in and available it won't get them. Obviously, if an emergency is taking place you should be available, but you'd do well to explain what *emergency* means. If someone needs you for such an emergency after hours, it ought to be to the level of an actual phone call.

It's not just for you; your people need to have boundaries too. Some of your team will answer your email or message at any time of the day or night if you put them in that position. Use the "schedule send" feature on your gmail and if you are composing an email "after hours", schedule it to go out during the agreed upon time frame.

If you don't establish communication protocols with your team, they will! And not collectively; EACH of them will decide what they like and deploy it. You will be inundated with communications and it will get away from you fast.

Here's a pro tip: you have someone in your office, a secretary, a receptionist, who is in that one place all day. YOU should not be in a place where people know they can find you; you should be, as we've established, in the building with the students and the teachers influencing their work. Instead of you being the "hub" of information, establish your support person for that role. In other words, when people want to know things, they don't come to you first; they come to your secretary.

If someone wants to see you, your secretary is in contact with you and will make sure you get the message and that you get there. If it's something immediate? She can let you know that too. You'd be amazed at how effective it is to let people do their actual jobs. That's what a secretary should be doing... supporting the administrative team. While you're on it, make sure that your secretary also has the keys to everything. You don't need to be in charge of everything; being the person that has to stop what you're doing and open doors or show the maintenance team the electric panel is not a good use of your time.

.. and deliver us from email...

Don't check your email all day long. Set aside times that you do so, but not constantly. Share your values with your team... make sure they know you're going to be in the halls and classrooms and that if they need you email your secretary. Encourage your people to communicate in person when possible, with text when more convenient, and with email if absolutely necessary, or to establish a record of some event.

You'll need to talk to the people who supervise you and are in contact with you from the Central Office as well. If you can make sure they know how to reach you when they want (through your secretary or a text to you?), it will keep you from checking email all the time to make sure you've been responsive with them.

Have you ever said at some time in your life about your job, " *they don't pay me to think?"* Well, in this job they do! And you should protect your brain like a dancer protects her legs or a baseball pitcher protects his arm. Your brain is your instrument. Don't wear it down with constant interruptions. Instead, *take control* of the communication flow. Don't be non-responsive; set aside times to answer email. (once every two hours would be enough and be a lot) Just not *all* of the time.

Part IV. Coaching

GETTING ALONG

You can make more friends in two months by becoming interested in other people than you can in two years by trying to get people interested in you.
~Dale Carnegie

Now that you're the principal, let's look at a big question: why did they hire *you*? Most likely the people who hired you noted your natural knack for building relationships. As the leader, you *also* want your faculty and staff to be great at relationships. Here's a challenge: what comes naturally to you *can* be hard for you to teach to others.

Here are ways you can help others in your school develop the kind of relationships that inspire everyone to do their best:

1.) **Talk about relationships.** It's important to ask your faculty about the fundamental nature of their relationships with students and with each other. The growth begins with a conversation.

2) **Encourage reflection.** Open the conversation about relationships, *then* ask your faculty and staff to reflect on their relationships. What are the products of their relationships? What kind of relationships do they have with students who do well in school? And, what kind of relationships do they have with those who don't do well?

3) **Prioritize ongoing growth.** If you think that relationships are important, you can bring attention to reflection and growth in relationships. Celebrate those who foster good relationships.

Create time for your teachers to recognize their colleagues who excel in relationship-building.

As the principal or assistant principal, if you want your teachers and students to be successful, you should be interested in their behavior and in the quality of their relationships. What people do and how they interact with each other is the definition of your climate and the strongest indicators of your culture. Like anything, your intentional focus in these areas is your best bet to get what you're looking for, and in building a school where people are successful and enjoy the experience.

Your job is more than just getting things accomplished. It's also about the manner in which you do so. As the leader, you set the tone for the others who work at the school. While it may not always seem that they hear what you say, you can rest assured that **they always see what you do.** Your actions can define your expectations for others at your school even more profoundly than your words.

That's reason enough to be intentional in the types of relationships you have with the others at school. How *do* you relate to your faculty? Your staff? To the students and their parents? Have you ever considered how much influence you have on others? When you interact with them, it's not lost in a vacuum, but it stands as your position paper on how you believe others ought to interact. The same holds true of your teachers with their students. Ever had a teacher yelling at a student because the student isn't being respectful? Yep. That's it. We often have no better place to begin making progress in our schools than within ourselves. I've mentioned to principals and AP groups frequently through the years, *the best way you can work on your school is to work on yourself first.*

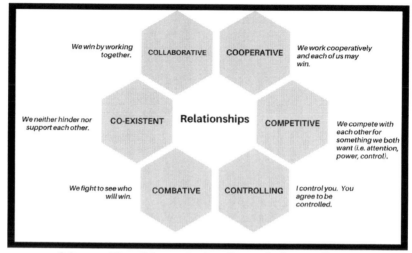

How Do You Work With Others?

Which of the following describes your model of interaction with others?

1. **Combative:** Your interactions are based on power. Your greatest tool in getting others to do what you want them to do is in making them do so.
2. **Collaborative:** Your interactions are based on an agreed set of circumstances or goals. Your greatest tool in getting others to do what you want them to do is in leading them to a common goal.
3. **Co-existent:** Your interactions are limited. Your actions may or may not link towards a common goal, but you exert little power or influence. There is little drama or glory in these relationships.
4. **Competitive:** Your interactions are based on a desire for achievement (being right, being better, being first, for example). While you may have similar goals, you have competing efforts to obtain goals.

5. **Cooperative:** You get along and you don't work against each other. That's much better than many of the other styles but not quite collaborative.

6. **Controlling:** Controlling relationships require someone who wants to control and someone who is willing to be controlled. There is an element of power and fear of reprisals in these relationships.

So, as a leader, how do you relate to the others in your school universe? Do you have differing types of relationships with different people? Why is that so? What type of relationships would be most beneficial for you to have as the leader of your school? What keeps you from having those kinds of relationships? Do you see the relationship between how you are relating to your teachers and how they relate to the students? What is your plan of action to become a relationship leader in your school?

OK, that's a lot to think about in one paragraph. But, we all talk about how relationships are always the key. If that's true, you as the school's leader should be intentional in how you relate to others. Before you can be intentional, you have to first be aware, and that will take some reflection and some conversations.

If this seems hard, and deep, well, it is. If you want to be the most effective leader you can be, it's not enough to tell people what to do and how to do it; you need to share with them why they should do it. Even that only goes so far. To truly **transform** an organization, you have to be a leader who helps people not only change what they do, but change **who they are.** To get there requires relationships operating with a deeper level of commitment.

Time to examine yourself and how you relate to others.

TALENT DEVELOPMENT

*Success comes in direct proportion to
the number of people you help.*

~Will Craig

Becoming a Principal can be a curious thing.

You get the job before you know the job, and then a big part of
your job is to figure out what your job really is.

Are you with me?

The expectations of the principal haven't changed over the years...
instead, they've multiplied! People still expect the principal to do
things they've done for decades-- be the face of the school, support
the students at extracurricular events, open car doors in the
morning and solve bus issues in the afternoon.

And.

And develop a comprehensive school improvement plan. And a
hospitable culture to rival Chick-Fil-A. And infuse STEM,
Mindset Training, and Differentiate for teachers and students alike.

That's just a sliver of all of the things you're asked to do, as you
know. But here's the challenge: out of the many important things
that you do, what's the most critical for you to do to live up to the
standards set for your performance? **Help your teachers grow.**

Yes, your responsibility for safety is always the most important thing you do, but the most critical for you to be deemed successful is to help your teachers grow.

It's for that reason everyone says you need to be visible. It's to help your teachers grow that you go to grade-level meetings, and PLCs, and book studies. It's the goal of your school's evaluation program. Our business is learning; our key representatives in the business are our teachers; their performance IS your performance.

Focus on talent development if you want your school to meet the needs of the students, because it's through your teachers that you reach out to each and every one of your students.

Your commitment to the task at hand-- leading your teachers in their professional growth-- is the pathway to success for you, your teachers, your students, and your school. Using the evaluation system as a support and as a needs assessment, your role as the school leader is to find out what your people need and get it to them. (Just as the teacher's role is to do the same for her students!)

I've heard school administrators tell their faculty members, "my job is to make your job easier," That's a notion worth a challenge. The truth is, the teacher's job isn't really easy, and while administrators offer support, our best play isn't to present ourselves as Tech Support or the Geek Squad. Perhaps our goal should be to be more like Mr. Miyagi from The Karate Kid? A trusted, wise coach whose wisdom matches up with his authority.

Making your teachers' jobs easier may be a lot to promise, but what if your focus is on helping your teachers find more meaning in their work? What if your "job' is to help them learn so much about doing their job that their confidence stands taller than their troubles and their doubts? That's a lot more substantive and sustainable of a gift.

BELIEF

*The most valuable resource that all
teachers have is each other. Without
collaboration our growth is limited to
our own perspectives.*

~Robert John Meehan

Science has proven what you probably suspected.

The number one influence in schools related to student
achievement is **what your teachers collectively believe about
your students.**

John Hattie and his team, using a meta meta-analysis have studied
the effect size of what works in schools. Hattie's work is
chronicled in his numerous books, conference speeches, and
papers, notably found in his book *Visible Learning.*

In a practical setting I've been posing this to the administrators I
work with: ***what do the teachers at your school REALLY think
about the students?***

> If the teachers REALLY believe that students can learn,
> that collective belief becomes who they are as a faculty.
> The opposite is just as true. If the teachers don't believe
> they can make a difference, regardless of what other
> initiatives you launch, *their impact will be limited.*

What Hattie and his team have done and updated regularly is a list
of factors (252 to be exact) related to student achievement and

their effect sizes. The higher the effect size, the more likely the positive outcomes on student achievement.

Ranking number one is **collective teacher efficacy**, defined by Hattie as the "collective belief of teachers in their ability to positively affect students."

Another way to look at it could be the "group think" of the adults in your school; that notion you've been working on since you've been in school leadership-- culture. Specifically, your school's culture around whether they believe that together, they can make a difference.

In your efforts to improve instruction at your school, are you building confidence in the heads and hearts of your teachers that they can do their work well, and together make a difference?

Part of your work as the principal includes observations, observation write-ups, and the evaluation process. Do the teachers truly see your work as a vehicle to help them be better prepared individually and collectively to make a difference for your students? Or, do they see you much like you view the fire marshall when they make an appearance at your school? (necessary but not necessarily welcomed)

The subtle difference of your work in the evaluation process can make a difference in the way that individual teachers at your school think about their work. This isn't a suggestion to "go easy" on your teachers in evaluation work: it's quite the opposite.

121

Teachers who get meaningful feedback and timely follow-up become more confident to do the work, and then begin to believe that their work can make a difference. That attitude spreads; if teachers think that your feedback is a canned response, rushed, or for compliance, its influence on their belief in their work will be limited if anything at all.

Think back to your days as a student. The teachers who challenged you are the ones who made the biggest difference in your learning. If you can challenge your teachers individually to be the best they can be as a part of a team of teachers that are on an important mission, you'll be amazed at how different your school can be. Like all good things, it takes time.

Where do you begin? With one teacher at a time, but in each interaction sharing a vision of what you can do together.

OBSERVATIONS

Mastery is achieved through deliberate practice.

~Karl Anders Ericsson

I need to work on my observations! Ever said this? Yes! You need to keep up and not fall behind in order to have meaningful performance conversations with your teachers and staff, but remember the observation is just the beginning.

It's like your dentist telling you that you have a cavity and then high-fiving you as you leave the office without any procedure. Observation is a form of diagnosis. It's not the treatment; you use it to inform your treatment design.

If you merely get your observation work completed without going further to help your teachers improve their performance, you are being compliant with the rules, but missing short on the spirit of the evaluation system... performance. And, you have a minimal number of minutes to dedicate to the process... you should work to spend them in the most high-leverage manner. And... the timeliness is critical; a performance observation should be followed up with a conversation as soon as possible, ideally same-day.

We should expect that our teachers do the same with the students... feedback and assessment review is most valuable when it's most timely. Let's be truthful... if you've been a school administrator for a number of years, you may have had access to a large number of Tier I teachers who were able to deliver adequate or better performance with a minimal effort on your own part. Maybe you've had a run of self-starters who are self-motivated, self-reflecting, and self-correcting. If so... be proud of yourself!

And be concerned about the next chapter. It's typical now that you have a larger number of teachers who need additional support to meet the adequate level of performance. It's ALSO true that our Tier I supports we've offered in the past probably aren't enough for today's Tier I. In other words, what we used to do to support teacher performance is likely to fall short of what they need today.

There WAS a day that hiring was the runway to launch your school's success; NOW, it's more likely that talent development is your path. As you've heard before, what got you here won't keep you here. With only a few exceptions, you would be wise to devote exponential additional time to teacher performance.

Maybe it's via instructional coaches, you and your assistant principals, or with other performance coaches. But here's the bottom line--- we have more faculty members needing more assistance than you have probably offered before, and just "doing observations" may not get you the teacher performance you desire.

COACHING FOR PERFORMANCE

Coaching is unlocking a person's potential to maximize their own performance. It is helping them to learn rather than teaching them.

~Timothy Gallwey

"Teacher support" covers a wide range of actions for the school administrator. It's appreciation, it's providing resources, it's creating positive environments, and it's also **coaching your teachers to be more effective in their work.**

Here are some things to consider when you are *coaching for performance, not for compliance.* Compliance has its place; performance coaching is a higher level of support. Think about athletics or the arts; parents seek out experts to deliver **specific performance coaching** to improve performance. Whether it's a piano teacher, a pitching coach for softball, or dance lessons, we DO know the value of expertise when it comes to coaching (and are willing to pay for it).

SO, think about yourself as a **performance coach** in those times you are working with your teachers *beyond the requisite evaluation cycle.* Here are some thoughts about **effective performance coaching** for your consideration in the hopes that you'll filter them through your lens of working with your teachers.

- **It's intentional.** Parents would hardly pay the big bucks they do for performance coaches if it wasn't *planned and purposeful* and part of the bigger picture of the elite performance you'd be seeking. Same goes for you as your teacher's performance coach; they usually don't find it very valuable when it's a hit and run. It DOES matter for climate building for you to drop by, but that's different than performance coaching. That means you know what you're going to do when you walk in their door. In his book, *Talent is Overrated,* Geoff Colvin shares that it's not just a volume of hours that makes someone an expert, but that the time spent on improvement is shaped by an effective coach, shaping *deliberate practice.*

- **It's individualized.** Gonna step on some well-intentioned toes here, but... when you say you're going to go around and observe <u>all</u> of the teachers on elements 2, 3, 7, and 8 of the evaluation system, that's great... but it's compliance. *IF you want to deliver performance coaching, what you do will differ from teacher to teacher. (and you can give yourself a pat on the back for standard 4, differentiation).* Your teachers have different needs. Developing a partnership through conversation with your teachers can help you collaborate on targeted areas for that particular teacher. An expert professional coach in other fields meets the learner where they are and leads them forward.

- **It's intense.** Not in the tenor or tone, but in the focus and timing. If you are going to coach someone, you attach *instruction to practice* to *reflection and review.* That time frame should be as succinct as possible if you want to REALLY improve performance. We do things in teacher observation and reporting that performance coaches would never dream of. Imagine having your child in tennis lessons. The performance coach you hire watches your child play, and then leaves, letting your child know that she will send a narrative and a rating electronically the next day. WHAT? That sounds ridiculous. It would only work if you were the fire marshall or the food safety inspector.

Those roles are important, but are NOT performance coaching roles. They are those of inspectors and rely on the *inspected* to have the expertise to correct the issues. Observe and MEET (not email or send in a platform!) with your coachee as soon as possible and definitely on the same day. How can we expect performance to be improved if the coaching is separated by time or mode of delivery?

Effective Performance Coaching: A Process

Here's a process for the performance coaching cycle... it's not THE process as there are many that can be of value to your teachers, but this one is something that's reasonable to do and provides ongoing conversation about the work of your teachers without the emotional parts (numerical ratings?) that can slow progress.

Performance Coaching
Short-Cycle Process

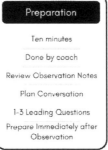
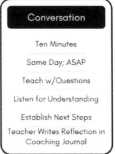

Observation	Preparation	Conversation
Ten minutes	Ten minutes	Ten Minutes
Priority Area Focus	Done by coach	Same Day; ASAP
Not for Evaluation	Review Observation Notes	Teach w/Questions
Area of Focus Pre-Determined with Teacher	Plan Conversation	Listen for Understanding
Keep focus on targeted area	1-3 Leading Questions	Establish Next Steps
Handwritten Notes	Prepare Immediately after Observation	Teacher Writes Reflection in Coaching Journal

It's easy to remember if you've ever worked to get your grass green and growing... it's called **"10-10-10"** a coaching cycle to help your teachers grow. Ten minutes of observing your teacher on a *specific part of her work* that you two have agreed upon she'd like to improve on. Ten minutes AFTER the observation for you to prepare for the conversation with your teacher.

THIS is the critical part; often school leaders don't slow down enough to plan their conversational process and the third part is hasty or non-planned. Think about what *questions* you want to ask your teacher... three is probably all you'll have time for.

Good questions, please, not "how did you think it went?" More like, "*which of your students were engaged most deeply in the lesson? why? which one's weren't and why?*"

Avoid "how many" or "what percentage" and help your teacher(s) focus on specific students... that's the work isn't it? After you've PLANNED the conversation, HAVE the conversation that day... at the very first opportunity. Measure the effectiveness of your coaching by seeing (on another visit) how well the teacher has employed your coaching. Sounds like a lot of time? It is! Quality over quantity?

Part V. Check Yourself

TIME

Efficiency is doing things right; effectiveness is doing the right things.

~Peter Drucker

One of my greatest privileges is to lead groups of principals and assistant principals in professional development. Part of that experience is the opportunity for our leaders to be together and to share concerns with others who understand where they're coming from. At least one-- and usually more-- of the principals immediately say *time management.* What causes you struggle as a principal or assistant principal? Time management.

In respect to that recurring theme, here's a list of **Five Truths About the Principal and Time Management.**

1. <u>You will never be "caught up."</u>

If you're an experienced principal, you already know this. If you're new or newer, you're learning it. If you are obsessed with having a clean desk, being completely caught up, and getting all of the items on your 'to-do' list checked off, being a principal can be a tough ride.

2. <u>It's Actually About Priorities, Not Time.</u>

While we talk about **time management**, it's really about **priority setting.** You can say anything is your priority, but you define what matters most in deciding where you spend your money and your time. If item number one is true (and it is, it's on the list of truths!) then the effective principal will focus here, on priorities. Your effectiveness is about the choices you make with your time more than it is the efficiency of your time, or the quantity of minutes/hours you work each week.

3. Spend Your Time Doing The Principal's Work

One of the common challenges that I often see with new principals is in their choice of what they do at work. Some new (and even some veteran) principals continue to do the work of the AP and don't get to the heart of the work of the principal. There are things that need to be done that ONLY the principal can do. Determine what those things are and make them a priority. No one else will ever get to them.

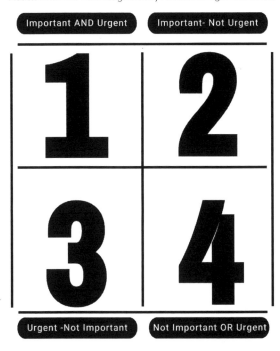

Time Management Matrix

Modeled from the matrix originated By President Dwight Eisenhower

4. If you don't spend time in quadrant two, who will?

The Eisenhower Matrix (crossing the axes of importance and urgency) gives us a framework in which we can measure the value of our choices with our time. We know that leaders should spend much time in quadrant two-- items that are defined as important but not urgent.

When I meet up with principals and ask them what they've been doing, I'm often saddened when I hear one say "you know... just putting out fires!" Admittedly, there is some of that must be done, but *if you're doing it most of the time, you're not doing it right.* In the **absence** of work done in that quadrant (planning, developing strategies, reflecting) then all that is left is urgency. You have to get here. Don't make excuses; get here or you'll be on the urgency carousel forever.

5. Quality Time is More Important Quantity Time.

Slow down and do things well. If you try to do too much-too fast, you'll begin to feel like you're not doing *anything* well. Also, this isn't a game that declares that the winner is the person who spends the most time at work.

Actually, that's not the trophy you want to win. It's much better to be the leader who gets *the most done in the shortest amount of time.* Be effective. Everyone is working hard, but the principals who are most effective are the ones who **are working hard at the right work.**

BALANCE

One day or Day One.
You Decide.

~Paulo Coelho

Steady. Calm, cool, and collected. Doesn't get flustered. Grace under pressure. Ice water in the veins. Keep it together.

There are a lot of things that people expect from their principal, but among the top things on the list is **the ability to exhibit steady leadership even when things are stressful.**

The principal has an enormous influence on the mood of others at the school! You can change the climate with your attitude on a daily basis. If you are bringing excitement, enthusiasm, and joy to your work it is contagious. On the other hand, if you're bringing an uptightness, nervousness, and uncertainty it too will spread to others.

The people at your school are counting on you to bring things into **balance.** To be a calm leader that brings confidence to others by being a consistently positive and steadying influence on the school's environment.

Here's the issue: that's a hard thing to do if *you are out of balance yourself.* It's not easy to steady the ship with wobbly legs!

It's like they tell you on the airplane... in the unlikely event of a loss of cabin pressure, oxygen masks will descend from the compartment above you...**please put on your oxygen mask before you attempt to help others.** This is something that as principals we don't always do so well with. Please remember, *bringing balance* to situations, people, and the operation of your school is an important part of the principalship; it's just hard to do if you are out of balance yourself.

Balance for the principal is about:

1. Spending time away from work with friends and family;
2. Spending time for your own relaxation, recreation, and renewal;
3. Focusing on healthy habits (sleep, diet, exercise)
4. Avoiding a preoccupation with school;
5. Developing strategies to manage stress.

When I work with principals, particularly new or newer ones, balance isn't always the first thing they focus on. Most of them believe they need to reach some level of efficiency before they can really get to that. The PROBLEM with that line of thinking is that when you're the leader who is out of balance, you don't perform at the same high levels of effectiveness as the leader who IS in balance. So, if you're waiting to "get caught up" before you get in balance, well... that is like the idea of "someday. "

Get balanced now. When you're out of balance, you are more likely to struggle. When you're not in a healthy place, you're more likely to be aggravated by small things. You are much more susceptible to illness (colds, etc..) Your decision-making suffers. Your interpersonal skills are diminished.

Don't wait for someday to get balanced, and don't fall into regret that you didn't do it yesterday. Today will be fine. Actually, today is the perfect day to reach towards the balance that can make you whole, and make you the awesome leader you were meant to be.

STRESS

The greatest weapon against stress is our ability to choose one thought over another.

~William James

In an article printed in *Harvard Business Review,* James Bailey writes about stress and how the leader can "combat its corrosive effects."

School leaders are under tremendous stress. As Bailey suggests, all stress isn't bad; stress can make you refocus, get tasks completed, and energize you for performance. That sort of "good stress" is only helpful if it's coming in small doses. That's why the effective leader learns how to ***manage*** stress.

You won't learn how to get rid of stress; that's impossible given the demands of school leadership. You also don't help yourself by pretending that stress doesn't exist or that you are immune to its effects. The effects are real, whether you acknowledge them or attempt to ignore them.

Here's the real story of stress: stress produces cortisol and epinephrine into your body. The neurochemicals can be toxic to your system and lead to high blood pressure, anxiety, depression, cognitive disorders, and a litany of other physical ailments if exposed for long periods of time.

When you have been under intense stress for an extended period of time? There's a reason you feel that way. When you work without ceasing and are preoccupied with work? That feeling you have is the chemistry inside of you. The effects of stress are real and often require treatment to address the damages done.

Bailey suggests that the steps towards renewal that counter stress can be sorted into **four categories :**

1. *Health:* You've heard it before and it's always true: diet, sleep, exercise.
2. *Removal:* Anything that gets you out of the struggle of work. Going to the movies, watching television, spending time with family, for example. Getting your body and your mind away.
3. *Intellectual Activity:* Puzzles, games, reading, studying history. When you study the world's greatest thinkers they often led such pursuits away from their main occupation. Lots of them were meticulous in their gardening.
4. *Introspection:* Meditation, prayer, breathing techniques, reflection.

The research suggests that it doesn't even take much time for renewal to begin, even 20-30 minutes can be helpful in renewing your body from the effects of stress. The difficult part for leaders? It needs to be daily.

So, develop habits that keep the real, physical, neurochemical effects of stress from hijacking the awesome person, leader, and individual that you are and that you can be.

LIFE-WORK BALANCE

...if you don't find a balance between your job and the rest of your life, you are doomed to burn out.

Chantal Panozzo

In working with principals, regardless of where it may be, one topic is always sure to stop the conversation and leave a pall over the room.

Balance.

We can pull off some amazing things as school leaders: juggle student requests, teacher preferences, and bus pickup/drop off times into an elegant, workable schedule. Teachers are marveled at how we can remember hundreds of student's names, favorite lunch spots, and cumulative tardies in our head with efficiency that Chat GPT would be envious of.

Principals can make it to a tennis match, Spring band concert, retirement reception, and an FFA Banquet all between 5 and 7 PM (and get a haircut during intermission of the band concert).

We have conditioned ourselves to schedule ourselves at a clip that seems like we are at more than one place at time. However, do we sacrifice being where we most ought to be to do so?

Chantal Panozzo posted a story today entitled "Living in Switzerland ruined me for America and its lousy work culture." In it, she gets to the root of our work/life balance issues: our cultural expectations of work. Principals and APs are products of those expectations, as well as unsuspecting promoters of this lifestyle to others around us.

At some point, your vision of what a principal must do was shaped by those who modeled it for you. You are doing the same now, for your assistant principal and others who are watching you.

Please know this isn't a suggestion that you slack off in your work. It is, instead, a reminder that one of the puzzles you should always be seeking to solve is that of balance. And, it's not just a self-serving quest. Simply put, if you don't find a balance between your job and the rest of your life, you are doomed to burn out. On the road to that, you'll become decreasingly effective, increasingly grumpy, and you won't be as good at your work as you have been. That's right, if you can't be convinced to seek balance for your own good, consider your work; it'll suffer if you don't take care of yourself.

At this time of year, principals and assistant principals (and teachers as well) face MORE to do rather than less. How do you get back in balance at such a critical time? This is actually the BEST time to do so. In future columns, we'll explore specifics on how to get yourself into balance, but for now, focus on a first step and move forward from there. One day this week, go home 15 minutes earlier than usual (which is still much later than normal people do!); turn texts and email off at 9:00 PM and keep them off until the morning so you can not only sleep but you can rest; and spend time with the people you enjoy, doing something that makes you happy that isn't school related.

Remember, someone is watching you now to see what principals do. Give them something to see that will help them be excellent in their work, but in their life away from work as well. They'll be the better for it and so will you!

7-1-1

School leaders need to give 7-1-1 a try before someone has to call 9-1-1 for them.

Mark Wilson

New principals...I was once like you. I served for fifteen years as a principal and assistant principal. I was committed to doing a good job and was going to make sure that if things weren't great, it wasn't because I didn't give it my all. I was willing to be up early and go to bed late as need be.

As technology evolved, just as you have done, I became more and more able to keep up with everything, all the time, from anywhere. (note; I love technology so please don't think I'm headed on an anti-technology rant) That allowed me to *physically* be away from school and still be in touch with anyone who needed me to solve their problems, answer their questions, or dispense permission, wisdom, or knowledge. I thought that would be great; I could be connected all of the time and still *be* with my family, friends, or away from school.

> Here's what I didn't realize; just because you are physically away from school doesn't mean that you are mentally and emotionally away.

When you are preoccupied with the school that you are leading (or any job you are doing for that matter) *you aren't leaving space for anything else.* We know from cognitive and neuroscience research that you need time and space so your brain can process. If you are preoccupied, you aren't providing that time and space. No matter how rockin' you think you are (and may actually be!), it will eventually catch up with you. If you practice moderation, you can manage it on your own. If you don't, someone else will have to do it for you.

In short, you can't think about school all the time. It's not just for your health (that should be enough) but it's also about your performance. The quickest way to get blind spots is to lose your perspective. You do so when you go in too deep.

Yes, you need to do a good job and this is going to take a LOT of your time; if it takes all of your energy, thoughts, and time it'll catch up to you at some point. Your performance will falter, your perspective will dim, and if severe enough, it'll affect your health.

It's not too late to fix it though! You need a hobby; you need time away; you need to put your phone/tablet/computer down for blocks of time. Practice 7-1-1 (7 hours of sleep a night, 1 day each week go home when normal people do, maybe 4-4:30, and 1 weekend day when you shut. it. down.)

Take care of yourself. We need you. Your school needs you. Your family and friends need you. Give your mind the rest it needs to be the leader and person you were meant to be.

HOBBIES

What's your hobby?

Please don't say *"I don't have time for a hobby,"* because that's going to lead to a lecture. Here's why the lecture: if you are going to effectively lead your school, you need to practice some life-work balance and part of that is some time for you. Hence, a hobby.

Joyce E.A. Russell, the vice-dean and the Director of the Executive Coaching and Leadership Development Program at the University of Maryland says that "finding time for ourselves is key to our own sanity." Russell shares that "having a hobby may be even more important to people who lead busy lives." That qualifies everyone who serves as principal and assistant principal for certain.

My brother Allen was a principal for the Sarasota County Schools in Florida for many years. As a role model for me as a school leader, I was always interested in what he was doing and how he grew as a principal. As a principal, he was known for many of the traits that effective principals exhibit --cool under pressure, unflappable, consistently bringing a stable environment for everyone on campus.

One thing I always noted about his work as a principal was his attention to **balance**. He consistently spent time with his family, his church, but he also always maintained a hobby. Every Saturday morning he had a regular group of friends with whom he played a round of golf. That Saturday morning ritual was as important as anything else he did in making him an effective school leader.

So, what is a hobby anyway? It's defined as a "pursuit outside of one's occupation," or **something that you don't have to do, but something you want to do.** This definition will disqualify some of the things that principals and assistant principals like to call hobbies.

You may enjoy attending your school's athletic and extracurricular events (I know that I did as well) but that doesn't qualify as a hobby. Spending time with your family? It depends. If you're referring to driving kids to practices or lessons, that's not the same as having a picnic or going bowling together. If you're having to rationalize that something you do is your hobby, chances are you really aren't getting the full benefit from doing it.

What does a hobby do for you? Researchers say that it lowers your risk for depression and dementia while contributing to an increase in your life expectancy. That's all. :-)

In the short-term, hobbies for school leaders give us a chance for social interaction with people outside of our school bubble, improving our perspective on things. Beyond that, and probably most importantly, *a hobby is a great way to reduce stress, get your mind off your work, and renew yourself.*

HOME

*Never get so busy making a living
that you forget to make a life.*

~ Dolly Parton

As the school leader, you are the person who is counted on to bring the universe around you into balance. You can't have favorites so you need to balance your work with faculty and staff. You need to balance the tasks that you have in your job. Both of these balance points are critical.

There isn't a balance point that is more important for you to get right as a leader and a person than this one though.

How well do you balance your time between school and home? Are you meeting a healthy balance between the time and energy you give to your job and the time and energy you give to those who love you at home?

This is a conundrum. You aren't going to be successful as a principal without working hard, giving of yourself to your school and spending long hours in doing so. That's just the truth.

The question is, *"at what cost?"* You need to do those things at school to succeed, but if you get your school/home relationship out of balance it will negatively impact all parts of your life.

All of us who work in these positions face this puzzle. How do we have it all? How do we take the limited resources of time and energy and distribute them between our work and our home in a

143

manner that leads to success, fulfillment, good results and great relationships?

I've said it before and will admit it again here: I don't think I was either the best or the worst at this, but I have learned some things I gladly share, not necessarily as an expert but as an experienced learner. Here are some things I've learned, some gleaned from personal experience, others from observation and also some from conversations with colleagues. These ideas may help you figure out how to get your life/work balance more balanced.

Notes On A Better Life/Work Balance

1. **Schedule Time and Make Your Appointments**: Save time for the people who love you at home and honor it just like you would an appointment with someone else. Do it regularly; do it weekly. Unless extreme emergencies occur, keep your "appointments" with loved ones and family.

2. **Balance Is Daily and Weekly, Not Just Annually:** We all can fall into the notion that we can make up for not being around a lot by spending a lot of time together when school is out on vacations. Those times can be great and make lifelong memories, but life is in the little moments that come along unexpectedly and in the flow of things. It's easy when we're working hard to lead a school to want to "make up" for lost time, but it really doesn't work that way. Balance is an ongoing endeavor.

3. **Make Your Work A Family Affair:** When your family is a "team" and you connect and collide on things at school together, you are able to create experiences and memories there too. Being together in your work is great and can make it all matter more. Sharing the importance of the work can make a difference too. If everyone in the family knows the importance of the work that you're doing, and also how important they are to you, the life/work balance has a different angle. If your family gets to celebrate the

successes of the school with you, it makes for a better dynamic.

4. **Don't Miss The Individual Time and Attention:** If you have a houseful of people who love and support you, congratulations! That's a good thing. It will, however, require you to plan out your time. You want to spend time as a unit, but you also want to spend time individually with the people in your family. Make sure you are making memories, sharing time, and getting to everyone.

5. **Never Forget What's Really Most Important:** When you leave your position as principal, they will get another one. With the exception of those individuals in charge when a school has been closed, everyone else who has left the position has had a replacement. Your job matters, but someone else *will* do it eventually. Your role as friend, spouse, parent, relative: that isn't something that is so easily replaced. Now, don't forget: your work is also a way to love and support your family. It allows you to support them financially. It also gives your family a good space to grow up in. Your job isn't an enemy unless you let it take you over. Remember who matters the most. You have pictures of your family in your office, not pics of your office at home. **Make sure they know they are most important.** They know that your job is going to require more time than most people who have "normal" jobs, but what they don't want to feel is unimportant. This is one of the most important actions you can take to balance life/work. Tell them how you feel about them. Take time with them and make sure they know how important they are to you.

There's no playbook to getting your life/work balance to be balanced, but the first step is to give it your attention. It's one of the most important challenges you'll take on.

LIVE WELL, LEAD WELL

Should we really consider it a badge of honor to say that, as an administrator we can't remember whether we ate lunch? If living well is just "what we do" at our school, imagine how that can positively impact morale, performance, and health?

What is the framework we use to guide us in our work as school leaders? In other words, **why do you lead your school the way you do?**

Most of us lead based on the experiences we've had. Sometimes we lead as we've been led, and other times our prior experiences teach us what NOT to do.

There's a part of the "how to be a school leader" narrative that we continue to perpetuate that you might want to reconsider. It's the framework that's based on: 1) working all of the time; 2) not recognizing or addressing the stress of the job; and, 3) falling out of balance with the other facets of your life.

We have seen this as the norm for principals and assistant principals for a number of years now, and it's time to consider another approach on *HOW* to be an effective principal.

That approach? **Live well, lead well.**

You can rightly assume that the reverse of this approach is also true: If you don't live well, you won't lead well. At least not for very long.

We can have more effective schools if we have more effective leaders, but you won't DO well unless you LIVE well. What does that entail? Let's look at five areas.

1. Bring awareness to Stress and Wellness;

What gets talked about gets done. If you want to have a culture of wellness at your school, talk about it. Talk ABOUT stress; not around it. Everyone has stress and teachers/administrators are no exception. The first step, as they always say, is acknowledging the problem, and we know that stress is a problem for teachers and administrators.

But, we also know that *wellness is a solution to that problem.* What would it be like if staff wellness was a cornerstone belief for your school or your system? How might that positively impact relationships between teachers and students? Teachers and other colleagues?

What good might the example of wellness bring to your students and your community? How might it directly impact the performance of teachers and of students?

So, here's the truth: you either have an intentional effort to focus on wellness, or you are just hoping for the best. The challenge behind that "strategy" lies within the increasing levels of stress reported by teachers and administrators. We need a better plan than to hope everyone makes it.

2. Establish Live Well/Lead Well as a norm, and not exception of afterthought.

The answer for staff well being is NOT a once-a-year promotion for losing weight. It also is not sponsoring a 5K in the fall. Random acts of wellness won't be enough; what we need is a sea change to help our people live well to lead well, on a daily basis. How can we partner with health professionals to teach our faculty and staff techniques to curb stress as it arises during the day? How can we support each other to have healthy habits both at and away from school? Should we really consider it a badge of honor to say that, as an administrator we can't remember whether we ate lunch? If living well is just "what we do" at our school, imagine how that can positively impact morale, performance, and health?

POSITIVE STRATEGIES

IN RESPONSE TO THE STRESS OF LEADERSHIP

HEALTHY ROUTINES	EXERCISE	DIET	SLEEP
ADDRESS THE STRESS	TEN MINUTES EVERY HOUR	WORK/LIFE BOUNDARIES	SOMETHING ELSE
MINDFUL HABITS	RESPONSE TO IMMEDIATE STRESS	QUIET TIME	RIGHT HERE; RIGHT NOW
IDEAS INTO ACTION	ACCOUNTABILTY PARTNER(S)	ONGOING EMPHASIS AT LEADERSHIP LEVEL	PLANNING ESTABLISHES DISCIPLINE

3. Lead by example from the system level.

The best way for a school to have an emphasis on wellness? Be a part of a school system that makes a priority of the well-being of its people.

Information on stress reduction can be shared with all of the employees across the system. Healthy habits throughout the day can be encouraged from that same level.

For the most impact, the effort to manage stress and promote wellness is collaborative, being fueled from the system level with engagement among those at the school.

4. Establish a framework of health habits; (expectations, timeline, reflections, and review);

All right, you've established a need for stress management and well-living; you've built a framework to make it work. Now what? What do you exactly do?

Some of your recommendations for living well at work might include: an educational effort on breathing techniques to reduce stress; an encouragement for movement; strategies to catch oneself when stress is building up. Your team might also encourage some exercises in gratitude, in recognizing other's support, and in activities to provide a respite from what might otherwise be a grind.

If you're thinking, "that sounds great but things are too busy here for that to work," you probably are a great candidate to build a healthier workplace! Remember, like everything you do in bringing about change, small steps lead to the biggest goals. Don't roll it all out at once, but bring about your change in stages, beginning with the most willing participants.

The idea of "living well away from work" holds even more possibilities. What might you and your team do to promote healthy lifestyles away from work? This effort might include awareness efforts (about exercise, hobbies, nutrition, and sleep) as well as group activities (teacher bowling night; running club) or encouraging your people to enjoy things with family, friends, or on their own.

Part of making this work is establishing that boundaries are normal and that technology shouldn't make any of us on call at all moments of the day and night. There should be provisions for real emergencies, but the fastest path to burnout for your teachers (and leaders) is constant mental engagement with work.

5. Establish accountability partners.

Want to do better? Make needed changes? Accomplish your goals?

You might want to consider the power of the **accountability partner.** As you begin an emphasis on stress management and living well, very few people will be against those ideas. However, very few people will be able to reach those goals without help. You'll provide lots of help: awareness/education about healthy habits; encouragement of making wellness a priority. The most significant help for any individual is in having someone to hold them accountable. A partner in wellness.

As you build your wellness efforts, imagine the ways that an accountability partner can be the key to success. Think of how you can acknowledge and recognize the efforts of the accountability partner. Develop a plan to connect people together in this way.

WORKING ALL THE TIME

Overworking leads to less-effective performance in pretty much everything that your job is all about.

If you're working long hours every day, taking work home every night, spending lots of your weekend doing emails and paperwork, and always feeling like you're running behind, rest assured you're not the only one.

Just because others are doing it doesn't make it any less damaging to you as a leader. You may be feeling the strains of all of those hours that you've been logging coming home to roost. Continuous overwork leads to fatigue, poor executive functions, inability to solve complex problems, issues with interpersonal communication and relationships, and shaky judgments.

In other words, overworking leads to less-effective performance in pretty much everything that your job is all about.

First, if you're working all the time and feeling out of balance, here are three reasons why you may have arrived at this destination:

1. You're Doing Too Much. One of the biggest reasons principals and assistant principals get overwhelmed is this one: they try to do too much.

When you have more to do than you can possibly do, and you aren't sure what ONE thing to do first, principals often try to do

151

EVERYthing. They end up not doing ANYthing particularly well, but they continue to try to have their fingers in everything.

Newly-arrived principals often do too much. Sometimes it's strategic so they can learn how things work; other times it's from not knowing who can be trusted to do things, and to do things well. This can be a transitional practice, but can't be sustainable.

Finally, there are some leaders who struggle with "doing too much" because... they *choose* to do too much! They operate from the idea that "the only way to make sure that it gets done right is to do it yourself." This wears the principal out and also develops a faculty who isn't prepared to think on their own.

2. **You're TOO Accessible.**

The modern-day leader has been told by everyone that you need to be accessible. That's true, but you can take it to an extreme and when you do, you make it difficult for you to be efficient and effective.

If you are available all day every day, and then again at night whenever people want to text, call or message you, you are too accessible.

The most efficient and effective leaders find the balance between being (and seeming to be) inaccessible and being overly-accessible to the point of harm. How is it harmful? If you're not careful, your folks develop a codependent relationship with you. If you're willing to do most of the thinking, lots of the problem solving and ALL of the decision making, people will let you. That's REALLY dangerous, because the more you operate that way, the less capable your team is to do those things (think, problem-solve, make decisions) and the MORE they will rely on you to do those things.

Don't go to the other extreme in an attempt to find balance; the answer lies in between. The answer does NOT lie in you doing all of the brain work.

3. **You've Developed Habits of Inefficiency.**

Often, BECAUSE you're doing too much, and BECAUSE you're too accessible, you inadvertently and often unknowingly develop some really inefficient habits. One of your challenges is this: you're at the top of the food chain at your school. Unless you have a coach, an attentive supervisor, or a really good mentor, it's EASY to fall prey to inefficient habits and have no one to prompt you to reflect and evaluate what you're doing.

The isolation of leadership can leave you ill-prepared to examine or alter your habits, and if they go unchecked for a while, they become your routines and eventually your beliefs. Beliefs are harder to change.

For example, I was visiting a principal who was so intent on listening in on what was happening in the adjacent front office that we could barely have a coaching conversation. Every person who came into the office and every interaction that the secretary was having stole the principal's attention. Over and again, people came into the office while we were meeting (some with a knock, some with an knock *while* they were opening the door). None of them were arriving with things that should have been tagged as "urgent."

What had happened there was this: EVERYTHING became urgent, and everything had to run through the principal, and it had gone on long enough that it had become normal.

During our coaching session we talked about.... you guessed it. How the principal was struggling to get it all done.

153

Regarding the struggle of workload for the current-day principal or assistant principal, despite the aforementioned you are NOT the problem. The world of education has continued to add on responsibilities to principals without additional support. What a principal does today is like a cumulative test… cumulative since we started having principals. We have continued to add to your plate without reducing things.

You may not have the authority to roll those things back, but what you *can* do is work on the specifics of your job. Focus on these questions:

- What can you do to make your job more reasonable?
- What can you do to be more efficient?
- Can you examine your habits to identify areas you can finetune?

I've got nothing but respect for what you and all of our school administrators do; if you can find a way to do it that keeps you from working all the time, it would be a victory for you and for your school too.

Part VI. Climate

CLIMATE BOOST

People will forget what you said, people will forget what you did, but people will never forget how you made them feel.

~Maya Angelou

School leaders want to impact **school culture** (the beliefs and priorities that drive the thoughts and actions of people in your school) ; they quickly find that culture is curated by faculty members. So, how do you influence the beliefs and priorities of your faculty and staff? A great entry point is climate.

Climate. Create an atmosphere that is conducive to change and receptive to growth. We will talk throughout the year about climate and how to make a difference in it at your school. Here is something simple but impactful: **Ten By Ten.** Ten compliments, to ten different people by ten o'clock AM. Every day, without fail.

If you share ten compliments every morning to begin the day, you will be setting the tone for your school everyday in a manner that will spread throughout your campus. A compliment can be a day-changer; it can go even deeper and be an attitude-changer! And, if several people are subject to such a change, well that means we have impacted the culture. Enhancing the climate is the pathway to changing the culture, and if you make "Ten By Ten" a priority, you will soon see dividends.

Let's focus on the compliments for a moment, remembering that all comments are not equal. The most important thing above all in the compliment business is **sincerity**. Only share a compliment when you mean it. Secondly, moving forward from sincerity is **focus.** If you compliment ten different people every morning for the same thing, that's good, but it could be better. Complimenting others is much like feedback for improvement as a part of our evaluation systems: the more specific the feedback, the better. Focus on what you see and what you say. *"Your work last night in putting together our science family event was great! Everyone I spoke to talked about how well it ran, how organized it was, and how much fun they had. Thank you!"*

Finally, if you want to excel in compliment sharing, be **generous.** If you get into the compliment business, you will be amazed at what you learn about the people in your organization. If you are sincere and focused in what you do, you will only be able to share compliments with those you know well enough. If you add the third element, generosity, you will have to get to know more of your people at a deeper level if you are going to be sincere and focused. This is the hardest part of being a good giver of compliments; you have to work at it to be able to spread it around to everyone, and if you are generous in your compliments, you'll want to spread it around.

So, before you become an expert (sincerity, focus, generosity), just get started! That part is easy... find ten different people, every day, before 10:00 AM, and share with each of them a compliment. As you're getting started, maybe your compliments will be at a basic level. That's fine! You need to begin somewhere.

Once you've gotten started, then work each day to improve in your 10 x 10 work, by giving compliments that are more sincere, and more specific to more and more people.

You'll be amazed at how much this simple act will improve your climate and over time, your culture, one compliment at a time!

INSPIRATION, INFLUENCE, IMPACT

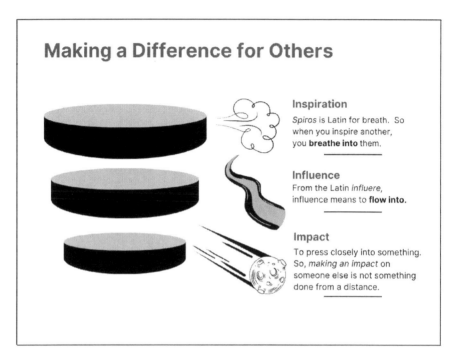

Making a Difference for Others

Inspiration
Spiros is Latin for breath. So when you inspire another, you **breathe into** them.

Influence
From the Latin *influere*, influence means to **flow into**.

Impact
To press closely into something. So, *making an impact* on someone else is not something done from a distance.

I *want to make an impact on the people around me.*

That's something that you might have stated as a goal for your work as a school administrator. So, how many people *can* you impact? This isn't just a parsing of words, but it's a critical understanding for you when you're leading a large group of people.

As you see in the image above, to *make a difference for others* you need a combination of approaches. Although we often say we want to impact others, by definition impact requires close contact. In our role as school leaders, it means not only proximity but *time.* Given the demands of school administration, you have a precious and finite amount of time, and you may have reasons to spread your time around somewhat evenly around the members of your faculty,

158

staff, students, and community. If that's what you choose to do with your time, it's excellent for other forms of difference making, but not specifically for impact.

How many hours does it take to impact someone else? It depends upon how *long-lasting* an impact you're hoping to make, the willingness of the other person to grow, and your skills. Obviously, the deeper the impact, the more time is required. But as an assistant principal, principal, superintendent, or director how many hours do you have to spend on *impact* and how many people can you reach?

To truly *make a difference* and lead someone to be more effective, to understand more deeply, or to care more genuinely about their work, your time commitment has to be regular, consistent, and enough. The numerical values for each of those vary but no matter what, if you're going to impact someone it's going to take a commitment of energy and time over a weeks and months if you want the impact to last.

So, how many people can you impact in the course of a school year? I've asked administrators in my classes that question for over a decade and the consensus is **fewer than five.** The actual number varies on the factors mentioned earlier, and

the choice of whom you want to impact; some choices may require more time than others. Impact requires ***coaching, mentoring,*** opening up to your mentee and them doing the same with you. It allows times for mistakes, reflection, review, and goal-setting. It takes commitment on both parts.

You have WAY more than five people to make a difference for this year, so what about them?

You impact some; you influence others; you work to provide inspiration for everyone.

While the scarcity of time prohibits you from *impacting* a large number of people, the savvy leader works to *influence* a larger number. Influence is to *flow through.* You can't be everywhere at one time establishing the values of the school, focusing on the mission, and gazing at the vision of the school. *That's* where influence becomes your conduit for success.

People in your school are behaving... non-stop. HOW they behave is why all of these things (impact, influence, inspiration) should matter to you. You have time to impact a few, but you have time to influence so many others. We most effectively influence others by demonstrating our values in real-life situations. Want to teach your faculty members to have grace under pressure? It's not going to happen in and email or a powerpoint. It's when they see you keep it together even when it's tough. Would you like for your teachers to treat their students with the utmost of respect? Those same teachers are looking at you for what the norms are at your school. If you yell at kids? They think it's okay for them to do it. If you're a smart-aleck and sarcastic? Fair game for them. If you are consistently a good listener, you're showing them how you'd like them to behave.

Influence, often through modeling, is the long-game. You seek to change a larger number of people while investing less individual time. Only those who are willing to be influenced are influenced; some, but not all, of those may benefit from more direct impact.

Influence isn't just what you do; it's obvious that the people you spend the most time with have the greatest influence on your behavior, for good or bad. Biggest influence on that new teacher you have? The teachers to her left, to her right, and across the hall.

What does that mean for you? It means you should influence the influencers. Some administrators work to do that through their leadership team. Whether you're able to accomplish the work there or not, you should seek to find others to spend enough time with on a regular basis so that you may be able to influence their thoughts about school and how it works. Less time than those you impact, but still a selective group. Who are the key people to seek? Those who have influence who are also willing to listen to what you have to share.

That leaves some people out? You do not have enough time to spend with everyone at your school to the point of impacting them. You also don't have enough time to spend where your modeling and conversations have much influence on your people. Selecting who specifically to focus on is an important task. You wouldn't possibly ignore everyone else, would you?

Nope. The answer is inspiration, "breathing into" someone. Breath is life, and when you're inspiring someone, you're giving them a little life. What does it look like? If you were asked to spend the next thirty minutes inspiring people what would you do?

It's more simple than you may make it. Our faculty and staff are *often* out of breath. The work they do each day requires heart and mind, body and soul. The inspiration they need is as differentiated as the number of faculty members you have.

Sharing a story or video (that we often label as 'inspirational') can reach some of your folks. Others are able to get a breath by taking their lunch duty when they are having a tough day. The leader shares inspiration and those in search of it find it and are refreshed by it.

MOTIVATING TEACHERS

Control leads to compliance; autonomy leads to engagement.

Daniel Pink

Daniel Pink, author of *When,* as well as *To Sell is Human* penned a book a few years ago that touches specifically on school, learning, and why people do what they do.

The book, *Drive: The Surprising Truth About What Motivates Us* is written in a conversational style, much like the works of Malcolm Gladwell, Chip and Dan Heath, and others. Pink collects the data, studies the meta-analyses, and then shares the findings in graphs, stories, and explanations that guide one's understanding of motivation.

Motivation, Pink suggests via the results of dozens of longitudinal studies , and how we respond to school as teachers OR students falls into three areas: **Purpose, Autonomy, and Expertise.**

As a practitioner and not a researcher, I found the premise to be highly applicable to teachers of most any variety. It begins with the absence of financial reward as a motivator, so that fits us well. Deeper, it suggests that people are motivated by doing what matters and helps others. Teachers are equally motivated intrinsically to do a good job and have expertise in what they do. Finally, if you have been an administrator for longer than five minutes you KNOW that teachers crave autonomy.

So here's the problem: if Pink's research and mine and your's (yeah, you agree, you know you do!) anecdotal observations are correct, and that our teachers line up with Pink's framework for motivation (Purpose, Autonomy, and Expertise) *we have not been feeding their motivation in recent years.*

EVEN PRIOR to the Pandemic, schools and systems have been on a long march towards *standardization.* On its face, that's not a bad thing. But do remember that there are *consequences for your actions and decisions.* Some of those consequences are favorable; others not.

What the move towards standardization has done is oppositional to Pink's premise. Do teachers have more or less autonomy today than five years ago? Are they able to have pathways that allow them to reach and validate expertise? Are they more likely today than five years ago to be not only told what to do, but how to do it? Again, any of those efforts may have been well-intended, but there's always fallout to be considered.

We talk A LOT about teacher shortage and the trickle of new teachers in our pipeline. School-level leaders are instructed to make efforts to retain teachers. Perhaps THAT'S one of the reasons for the interest in strict interpretations of student conduct issues. If we aren't feeding our teacher's motivation for purpose, not giving them the autonomy to create and solve things, and not appreciative of their mastery of their work, then it's *only natural that they are more likely to be bothered by things that otherwise might not seem as important.*

People who have aspirations and are working on them regularly are less likely to be sidetracked by other things. Engage your teachers if you want to engage your students.

HEALTHY URGENCY

A higher rate of urgency does not imply ever-present panic, anxiety, or fear. It means a state in which complacency is virtually absent.

~ John P. Kotter

Being a principal is a GREAT job; you can make a difference in the lives of lots of people, kids as well as adults.

Being a principal is also a DIFFICULT job; you find yourself in the middle most of the time.

The people who have entrusted you with the helm of the school rightfully expect that under your leadership there will be academic success. You don't teach classes anymore; your path to influence academic performance comes in your connections with your teachers.

You always face this target: finding the right balance to **establish a positive workplace + raise expectations of performance.**

To make it more interesting, the climate/expectations graph looks a little different for *each* of your teachers.

Please remember this: **there are consequences to actions.** Some consequences are positive and intended; others can be negative and unintentional. Your actions DON'T live in a vacuum. Something happens and it may even affect your people disproportionately.

As you lead your school, it's easy to **be reactionary** to outside influences (mandates, new programs, pressure). You can do what you like... but there are going to be consequences of what you choose to do.

It's easy to underestimate the influence you have on the people of your school. You THINK they don't hear you, but they do. They hear you through your tone, your body language, and your words. They see your actions and see what matters the most to you. They feed off of your energy and your vibe.

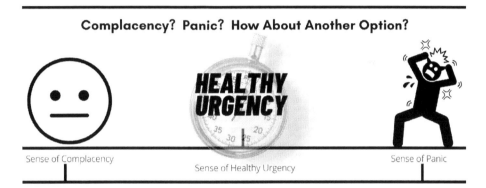

Complacency? Panic? How About Another Option?

Sense of Complacency

Sense of Healthy Urgency

Sense of Panic

If you aren't careful, you can lead your faculty into a **sense of panic.** That may lead them to behaving chaotically, and that's not their best suit. Watch your words and your body language. There are consequences to creating a sense of panic.

On the other end of the scale is a **sense of complacency.** It's just as bad. If your people feel defeated, uninspired, don't care... you will find success elusive.

Between the extremes is a better place... where people feel a sense of **healthy urgency.** Not panicked... not checked out. Working with passion but within control. Confident in their abilities and committed to the work. THAT'S where to be. As the leader, how do you get them there?

In pursuit of healthy urgency...nine things to know

1. Our brains are hard-wired against it. The amygdala recognizes change as a threat and does its fight-freeze-flight thing when change is presented. Your body tries to protect you from change. Let that sit for a minute.
2. According to a 2019 research study, teachers identified themselves as risk-averse at a higher percentage than most professions.
3. Members of a group (like... your faculty!) vary in their reaction to change.
4. The more people who are affected by a change, the more time needed to prepare for the change. (like moving the car pickup line needs time and lots of communication since it involves a large number of people.)
5. Your teachers are more likely to implement the change effectively if they are involved from the beginning (at the idea phase). Implementers that are involved in the creation are much more effective.
6. You don't need everybody on board to bring about change. Statistically speaking, we have around 16% of a normally distributed group that are against most change. We ALSO have that same percentage of our folks with "factory settings," ready for the excitement and potential of change. It's the 68% in between that determine the success of any idea, so the leader who focuses on the willing is more likely to reach success.
7. When possible, consider bringing about change in phases. When you are able to start with a "coalition of the willing", THEY can be a part of influencing others to consider the change.
8. Change is more readily launched when your teachers have developed trust in you as the leader and among themselves.
9. REAL change takes time.

RECOGNITION

A person who feels appreciated will always do more than is expected.

~Amy Rees Anderson

When you make it to the end of your first year as principal, you will have such a great feeling of accomplishment. Everyone always feels better when they can get all the way to the end. No more unknowns! You are ready to roll it back, this time with an extra helping of confidence and some knowledge you didn't have before.

Before this year is in the books, there are still some things left to do. Among the most important that remain are your year-end events, ceremonies, and celebrations. Awards night. Honors ceremonies. The academy awards of your school!

 Never underestimate the importance of these commemorations. Make sure you are an **active** participant in these events. Here are a few reasons why.

1. **Year-end events reveal the culture of your school**. What you take time to recognize, you must really value. So, the content and structure of these events display for everyone to see what you really believe is important. Have you focused on positive behaviors this year? Now is the time to reflect that with your year-end award presentation. If it's citizenship that you want, make it a part of what you honor at year's-end. Be intentional with

your award ceremonies to highlight the work of those who have focused on what you had hoped they would.

2. **Year-end events demonstrate the level of your expectations of excellence**. Every event answers the question "who are we?" It is a reflection of you as the leader and the level of pride your school has in what it does. The intentional leader makes clear the expectations of what it will look like at her school, and helps teachers and staff in shaping their events to meet those expectations. While it is not your role as principal to be the event planner or master of ceremonies for everything that happens at your school, you ARE responsible for setting the tone of what others will do. Without some direction, results may vary. What do you want these events to say about your school? You certainly want them to demonstrate a high level of professionalism. You want them to run smoothly, to be advertised well in advance, to be quality events. Don't expect everyone to read your mind on what you are after; clarify your expectations and make sure that those who organize these events know that you want them to speak well of your school. (Use your Plan-Brief-Implement-Debrief protocols!)

3. **This is a great opportunity to show the world the good things that are happening at your school.** Take pictures. Publish in your local newspaper. Blast it out on your school's socials. You can be posting pictures of award winners on the school's Instagram account well into the summer if you want to! Again, this is an opportunity to share the work of individuals but also the beliefs of your school. Plan it in advance. Always have someone in charge of photography. Plan your follow up and coverage before the event begins.

4. **Don't Underestimate The Value of An Award .** As a high school principal who believed in recognizing the works of our people, I can tell you story after story of appreciative parents and students who were excited beyond words to be recognized. These

168

things matter. This is an opportunity for us to bring families, students, and our school together in this moment of celebration. This is one of your most important acts of the entire year. Smile broadly in every picture. *These* are the events that you should stay late for. Don't be in a hurry to get everyone dismissed and move onto the next thing. Let them savor it, while you savor it yourself. This is the fruit of all your labor; don't be quick to let it go. Bask in the glow and let the positive energy fuel your next quest.

5. **This is a personal reflection on you, your beliefs, and your leadership.** Everything that happened at your school should demonstrate a subtle sense of excellence. Make sure that there are ferns on the front of the stage. Have a tablecloth with your school's insignia drape the table where the awards await the recipients. Print and distribute programs of the event for everyone's scrapbooks, their drawers of awesome things, and other places where such important things go.

Make sure that the sound system works and that you have a back up if it doesn't. If you don't have a great sound system, now is a good time to find someone in your community to volunteer to bring *their sound system* for your award ceremony. Use all of your resources to make this a moment that will be a great memory for all those who attend.

Like a lot of things, if it goes well there are lots of people to thank and to give the credit to. If it doesn't go well, well, you know who gets the blame. There's no substitute for the planning that you can do right now to make sure that these events meet their potential and do all of the good that they can do. Enjoy planning these events to be the wonderful once in a lifetime thing they are intended to be.

Part VII. Leading

ATTITUDE TOWARD LEARNING

A bad attitude is like a flat tire. You can't go anywhere until you change it.

~Steve Keating

Attitude Check

Above the door leading into the Professional Learning room of a school I was visiting was a sign that greeted participants with this question:

What attitude do you bring to today's learning?

It's a great question to pose, as it forces its readers into a brief moment of reflection about their approach to the learning that awaits them on the other side.

After Further Review

After the visit and while riding around the hills and plains of Georgia, further reflection led me to ponder a different question, one that wasn't posted or printed, but one that made me go hmmm?

Shouldn't educators be passionate about learning without a sign to remind them?

The sign about attitude on the PL room door... I didn't ask, but I'm guessing that it was put there either to prevent visibly-bad attitudes about learning OR in response to such attitudes in meetings past. I've been around professional learning for decades, so it's not shocking to think that teachers (or administrators!) might be less than enthusiastic about some learning, but despite that acknowledgement, it's still disappointing. How can we get our students to be passionate about learning if we aren't passionate about it first?

It's probably easy to contend that while we may not always be passionate about all professional learning, we can still be enthusiastic when in the role of teacher, particularly if we enjoy that content more. But here's the problem with that line of thinking: the students may find the content intended for them just as uninspiring as the content from the PL room that the teacher didn't engage with.

Passion For Learning

Here's a question to consider: When you learn a passion for learning, isn't everything else easier to learn after that?

Our students would be well-prepared for their next endeavor if they left their class at the end of the year, full of curiosity, a thirst to know things, and a satisfaction in the process and product of learning. Truth is, we don't spend enough time on those things, but what if we did? Would our students approach their learning differently? Would the content we share be more readily mastered if we taught the value of learning before (and during) our specific instructional goals?

Back to the PLC Room

Let's connect the classroom back to the PLC Room with this question:

Are your expectations of passion for learning higher for your students than for your teachers? We have PLCs and other groups and teams of teachers all across the land who value learning, believe in collaboration, and treasure the opportunity for learning with their colleagues. There are a lot of these teachers and administrators in schools and systems all over the map. There are, however, teachers and administrators who don't feel that way.

How about at your school? How passionate about learning are your teachers? How passionate are YOU about learning?

When you are leading learning with your faculty, are you modeling quality, impassioned instruction? PLCs and professional learning ought to be fun. How is adult learning normed at your school? What percentage of the time that your adults are in learning settings are they sitting and listening, and what percentage of that time are they talking, sharing, and doing?

One of your most important roles as the school's instructional leader is to set norms for learning. Is the learning you facilitate with your teachers engaging? Are you passionate about it? Do you work to create a great learning experience with your teachers?

Good Goes Around

Teachers with a passion for learning tend to lead classrooms that foster that same passion. The principal and administrative team can fuel and foster that passion by leading professional learning and PLCs that circulate a love of learning among all its participants. When that passion becomes the norm, your teachers will race to get INTO professional learning and their PLCs rather than to race OUT. When you establish THAT culture about learning, you will thrive not only in PLCs but in your classrooms across the school.

And then you can take down the "what's your attitude..." sign.

174

EMBRACE FAILURE

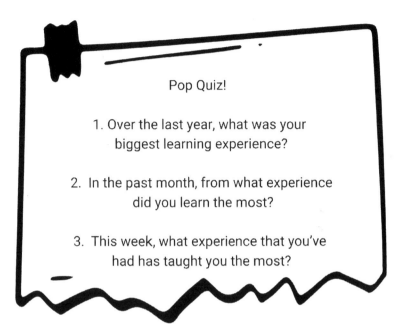

Pop Quiz!

1. Over the last year, what was your biggest learning experience?

2. In the past month, from what experience did you learn the most?

3. This week, what experience that you've had has taught you the most?

Times up. Pencils down. Thank you. Now, did you mention mistakes in any of your answers? Did any of those learning experiences begin with *'this was the easiest thing I've ever done'*? Perhaps you found failure first, and then success?

Perfection is the enemy of progress. If you are obsessed with never making mistakes, you'll be reluctant to experiment, to try new things. You'll instead stick with only things that you've done before. Again, this is not an invitation to be reckless. That's not a good leadership strategy. Neither is making the *same* mistakes over again. Leadership is learning, and learning is doing. And doing means that you have an opportunity to learn from your mistakes.

Here's where this advice is born: I've worked with many leaders who *dearly struggled* with making even the smallest of mistakes.

Their self-worth became in question. They withdrew into themselves. They were embarrassed and ashamed.

None of that is a badge of honor. You are *going* to make mistakes if you're a principal. NOBODY finishes their work as a school leader undefeated. In fact, probably no one finishes *a day* as principal undefeated. You have so many decisions to make and so many interactions with other people that it's statistically implausible to bat a thousand.

So what do you do with those mistakes? Don't let them pass through your day without reflection and refinement. You begin your day with 1-2-3 (one thing that brings you hope, two things you hope to accomplish, and three people for whom you'll help bring joy). To help you learn from your mistakes, try *ending* the day with 3-2-1.

Find a journal of your liking, and end the day with these reflections. Three things you learned today; two questions to contemplate; one goal for tomorrow. This process helps you identify your mistakes and address them on your own terms.

Some of the mistakes you make will be subtle. You'll recognize someone publicly at a meeting and later find out they were mortified to be put in front of everyone. You can't go back and undo it so what do you do? This is how you grow. You make that one of your questions for the day. *How could I have prevented that from happening?* Here's the fun part: you don't even have to come up with all of the ideas. Pose that question to your administrative team or your wise councils. They will surely have (or Google!) an idea to sample the *love languages of work* that your faculty most enjoys. Then, you learn, and you grow, and you move forward.

Some mistakes aren't even looked at in those terms. They are looked at as <u>progress.</u> Have you ever used the multi-surface cleaner *Formula 409*? Did you ever wonder how it got its name?

According to the Formula 409 Website:
*409 is **not** the area code where the formula was first concocted or the number of bacon strips the inventor had that day. Creating the ultimate cleaner doesn't happen on the first try. And it didn't happen on the 101st or the 301st either. It wasn't until the 409th batch that they (the Detroit Inventors) were finally satisfied. And so, the name stuck. Formula 409. True Story.*

My favorite part is <u>*creating the ultimate cleaner doesn't happen on the first try.*</u> Of all organizations, we should embrace that notion… that excellence doesn't happen on the first try. That we have to work again and again to reach a place where we've succeeded. If the culture of your school is that productive struggle is embraced, you'll see more people try more things. If it's one where mistakes are met with admonishments and reprisals, the people of your school are going to unplug their creativity, throttle back on their enthusiasm, and primarily attempt only the things they already know how to do. Not a rousing place of experimentation and wonder.

To make embracing mistakes a part of your school culture begins with you. What YOU do as the leader sets the pace for what everyone else does throughout your school. I've not yet run into an innovative school with an afraid-to-be-wrong principal.

Don't you want your teachers to lead engaging explorations of learning? Don't you want your students to be persistent and keep trying through their errors? Then as the leader, set the stage! Shift from fearing failure to celebrating discovery. The 409 story is an example of the celebration of discovery. If they'd been easily set back by "mistakes", there'd been no discovery.

To elevate the performance of a school, you first have to elevate the conversation. If the people of your school (teachers, staff, students) primarily think and talk about esoteric topics (dress code, duty, homework, etc...) what are they NOT talking about?

Schools that excel talk about igniting curiosity... the journey that learning truly is... they talk about progress.

What do you talk about at your school?

VISION

Your teachers make 99% of their decisions regarding instruction, assessment, and interaction with students outside of the presence of their administrators.

When people get new jobs in education, it's understandable that they tend to gravitate back to their previous ones early in the transition. That's why many new principals do a lot of assistant principal work out of the gate. It's something that you'll want to work your way out of as quickly as you can.

Reason being, there is *principal work* to be done that can only be accomplished by… the principal. One of those duties is that of *communicating, clarifying and serving as guardian to* **the vision.**

Let's talk about *vision* for a moment because, frankly, so many people get vision and mission transposed. It's much more than just semantics, it's a critical understanding that is one of the things successful principals spend much time and energy on.

To understand vision, let's begin this way. As the principal, you lead a particular number of faculty and staff members, *whose work determines your success as a principal.* Your effectiveness comes down to, in many ways, how effective you are in helping them understand _what to do_ and _in what manner_ it's done at your school. So you'd think, _I should spend a lot of time with my people to see how it's going._ You've heard that presented this way, no doubt: _you've got to inspect what you expect._ That sounds really good... except it's only minimally effective.

Here's why. Let's say you're going to "inspect what you expect" to the tune of one hour per week for each and every one of your teachers. That would be good, right? More than you think your school did while you were assistant principal? Anyway, one hour --- sixty minutes-- in each teacher's classroom every week ought to be valuable in supporting their work?

Assuming that your teachers are interacting with students six hours a day for a 180 day school year, that would be a total of 1,080 hours for the year. _If_ you, the principal, could spend an hour per month with each of those teachers, that would be a total of 10 hours for the year.

Based on observations and conversations with hundreds of school administrators, an hour of in-class observation every month for every teacher would be a goal we would be proud to achieve. If you were able to do it, here's how the math of it looks: it would represent _less than one percent_ of your teacher's school year with students. What that means is that each of your teachers are _on their own_ to make decisions regarding instruction, assessment, and interaction with students for **99.07%** of the school year. _So much for "inspect what you expect._ Let's say you got very effective and efficient and did twice that... two hours a month, every month for

180

every teacher. Now you would have gotten the time they are doing what they do without you down to… **98 percent.**

According to research conducted by *Teach Thought*, a teacher makes an average of 1,500 educational decisions a day. Given they are on their own without you around 99% of the time, that means they are making 1,485 of those decisions without you around. Perhaps a better mantra would be, "make sure they know what you're wanting from them in the classroom because they're going to do almost all of it on their own."

You have to be strategic in how you train your teachers on WHAT to do but equally HOW to do it. You have precious little time to do so, which is why you spend as much time as possible out there where they are. The whole place is a classroom for you to teach *what and how* to your teachers… so they'll make good choices in that 99% of the time when you aren't around.

There's not enough time for you tell them everything so you try to make up a lot of ground by helping them to understand where we're going, what we're hoping to accomplish, and the manner in which we want it done.

That's why you want to be really good… an expert… on **vision.**

When I do work with schools and school leaders on vision, I ask them to bring in a picture. No words, a picture. When we're working with vision and mission, here's an easy way to clarify: think about a **visionary** (someone who can see potential, and what it can look like in a future setting) and a **missionary** (someone, as a part of a common calling, is working to lead others to action now).

Your teachers are on their own over 99% of the time with their understanding of the vision to guide their mission. If they don't understand it? They'll be second-guessing themselves. Maybe they won't be willing to risk being wrong if they're in a school of show instead a school of grow? THIS is a major impediment to school success. Failing to dedicate adequate time and energy to the school's vision, mission, values, and purpose is the pathway to failing as a school. .

The most effective integrations of vision into the school's culture come from an intentional exploration and coming together around a collective vision. *Only those who are a part of the creation of the vision will have a deep understanding of what it means.* For that reason, **every year,** schools and school systems should renew their commitment to the vision and mission, to values and purpose. It's easy to become enamored with what we do in that work, but the best work is done in pencil and never laminated. The obsession shouldn't be in getting a perfect or attractive set of statements, but in the value in what these statements can provide in the absence of explicit directions and immediate supervision.

For example, when we say *all students can learn* (and most everyone says that), what does that actually mean in the classroom? Does it mean that when a student does really poorly on a test, that we develop a plan with the student for her/him to learn missed material and retest? Does it mean that a student who wants to be in an advanced class gets to be in it, or do we have some sort of qualifiers that permit/deny admittance?

As the principal, you spend your time leading your people into examining real-life school situations through the lens of your vision, your mission, your values and purpose. You build VMVP together during the off-season (post-planning, Summer, and/or pre-planning) You examine them continually. You review them intentionally, and always return to them with new members of your team as well as all of the veterans. As Brenc Brown says, *clarity is kindness.* Having a clarity of what you're doing in your job makes it much easier to approach. Shouldn't the people who work at a school be able to reply when asked, *what are you all working on here? What are you trying to accomplish?* The clearer the answer, the more focused the work, and the more focused, the more likely to achieve what you're after.

To the person who doesn't know where he wants to go, there is no favorable wind.

~ Seneca

By the Way, Don't Leave Your People Guessing

People in general aren't big fans of uncertainty and ambiguity. Teachers, as a subset of people in general, REALLY dislike those things. Most teachers by definition are planners. They like to understand what's happening, when it's happening, and how long it lasts. Most teachers don't like surprises (unless they're chocolate) and prefer to have the plan shared with them in advance, in writing, and in short-form.

There are *many* things that arise during a school year that can't be foreseen, and most of your teachers will offer you grace for those things. But, if you are consistently doing a lot of last-minute reveals and frequent same-day changes, you may lose some of the confidence you've earned with your people.

You need to spend a lot of time thinking about a year from now, six months, three months. But you ALSO need to forge that thinking into action and have clarity about what's happening next month, this month, next week. You need a sort of "split-screen" view, like those fancy televisions that you can watch more than one game at a time.

Beyond logistics, the desire for clarity extends into understanding what you're trying to accomplish and why. One thing I learned (after having gotten it wrong enough to want to try something else) is this: as the principal, you don't have to have all of the answers. The more you involve your people, not just for advice and consent, but for original creation, the better your school operates. At one of the schools I led, I had a couple of teachers who always seemed to find my mistakes when I roll out a special bell schedule. After realizing their skills with details, I asked them to do the next bell schedule when we needed it. If they were going to crunch through it all, why not ask them to do it from the start?

Understanding that your people desire clear and timely communication about the who/what/when/where/why and how MUCH MORE than they want a principal who does everything is an important step towards effectiveness. And, the humility you show in doing so is the right kind of humility for the school leader.

184

FOCUS

Your teachers will get worn out if you try to make everything a priority, so determining a focus... and shifting smoothly when it's the right time to another focus... is a skill of the effective principal.

As the principal, what's my job? To talk about vision: <u>what can be</u>. To share expectations: <u>how things should be done.</u> And, focus: <u>What do we do right now?</u>

Think of yourself as a lighting technician at a theater. You are in charge of the spotlight. When the stage lights are all on, anyone can look anywhere they'd like. But when you dim those lights and turn on the spotlight... you get to determine what everyone looks at.

One of the many roles of the principal is that of spotlight operator. You first dim the lights in the corners and in areas that you don't want people to spend their time on. Then, you put that spotlight right on what your team needs to focus on to be successful. If you *don't* spotlight something, you are taking a chance and just hoping that people will look at the right thing. When the stage lights are on, everything seems to be of equal importance. When you put on the spotlight, that's going to get attention.

Here's where it gets difficult. What *should* you select to spotlight? What should be the focus?

As the leader, you'll find yourself moving that spotlight around quite frequently throughout your tenure as principal. Sometimes the focus needs to be on safety. (Safety is always important, but sometimes it is *the* focus) On other occasions, it's instruction. Still, at some times you'll need to invest your time and energy in Social/Emotional Learning.

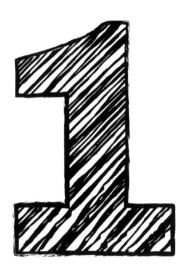

There are always more important things to do than can be done, and all of them can't be the *number one* priority. In fact, as Gary Keller reminds in his book *The One Thing*, that's the correct spelling. Priority. It was meant to be singular and stayed that way for over five hundred years. Only in the 1900s did people begin to make a word that literally means 'first' into multiple firsts.

Schools are notoriously called upon to do more things than they have resources to do. As the principal, obviously, you can't just do one thing. We always have multiple things to do. But, your teachers are watching where you spend your time and listening to your words. *What gets talked about gets done.* So what must get done? What *should* get done? How will you bring enough oxygen to both?

That's one part of your role with focus, helping illuminate the priority for the school. There's another part, and it's about you. Your own focus. Which leads to …

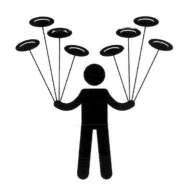

My goal as a "principal coach" is pretty simple… help school leaders lead schools. What I've learned is that **focusing on the right work** is one of the most critical pieces of success for principals. We've been conditioned to think that 'working hard' is the answer; it's necessary, but *working hard at the right work* leads to better outcomes.

In hundreds of coaching relationships I've been a part of over the past years, I've noticed several problem areas that keep surfacing. One of the most prevalent ones is the *do-it-all* principal. So many new principals have difficulty in determining what their job is and what it isn't. If you don't get the principal's work done, there's no one around to do it for you, so it goes undone or ends up being something you do when you *ought* to be resting, spending time with family and friends, and the like.

Nearly every new principal struggles at some level in figuring out "the job." There are parts of it that are only clear to you when you are in the position, and not things you can easily anticipate. What truly paralyzes a principal is when their exploration of what the job is about begins with doing *everything*.

To be clear, if you try to do everything, you won't do *anything* very well. There's just too much to do. And, beyond that, it's not good leadership. Your worth as a leader is measured by what *others* do, not only in what you do. Your legacy begins on your first day at the job. It's then that you begin to build capacity for life *after* you no longer work there. That's right. Many people begin to think about legacy at the end of their tenure; those who leave the strongest legacies are building them from the beginning.

When you leave your principalship, they'll hire someone else to replace you. (Shocking, I know!) When that person comes in, chances are in some form or fashion, they'll ask the people who remain (your teachers, your staff, students, parents) *what they think they should keep doing, what they should stop doing, and what they need to begin doing.*

Do you know what they'll want to keep? *The things that they built from the ground up.* Do you know what they'll want to dump? *The things that you kept to yourself.*

And, if you asked them some version of those same questions, that's very likely what you got as well, but in reference to your predecessor.

If you try to do it all, you neither build capacity nor loyalty for your ideas or your work. If you lead, however, you'll be amazed at the shift that happens. It becomes what _we_ *are doing* when your teachers talk about the work. That's more than a subtlety; it's a fundamental piece of how your school will grow and function.

EXPECTATIONS

Around 65-75% of your people, coalesced around a set of values and priorities is enough to have an exceptional school. Those in the 25-35%, find it harder to be the influencers they once were. They are most likely to acquiesce or relocate. (Negative people really seem to hate being around positive people!)

I've worked with school systems where the gentlemen wore suits and ties and the ladies wore business dress every day. I've also worked with systems where a collared-shirt was dressed up and I could see a clump of smokeless tobacco in the mouths of some of the people in my workshop.

Norms vary. Not just in dress, but in… well, nearly everything. Norms relate to school administrators, teachers, and to students and they answer the question, *how do we do things around here?*

Norms and expectations, given time, become the culture of an organization. When a new leader comes to a system or a school they listen to find out what the norms and expectations are, and what the culture of the system or school is. Often, they've been given instructions by the people who brought them there to change the culture. Your first step is to find out what expectations are driving the actions of the people of the school now.

In the absence of clear expectations, people tend to choose their own. People in a group tend to gravitate to the mean and behave with the general expectations of the group. Meaning, you may have some people who want to do better but it is exceptionally difficult when they're swimming against the tide.

When you have enough people who are willing to honor new expectations, you work with them to help deepen their understanding and their commitment. They begin to influence those around them and, with time and consistency, begin to create a new average, and a new norm.

Your initial time is best spent with those who are ready for higher expectations. Building a *coalition of the willing* is the pathway to creating new norms. Those who are ready don't take as much of your energy to get started, and actually give you positive energy back though their enthusiasm.

It takes more energy to start with the unwilling… schools are too heavy to push up from the bottom… try pulling them up from the top. Your willing people are reinvigorated and their attitude begins to pull a few others their way.

Not only do you think about *WHO* to work with first, you focus on *WHAT* to begin with. Don't try to change too many expectations all at once. Don't try to change things too quickly. Change has its own timer… the best of leaders learn how to read it.

Choose expectations that are attainable. Like battles, choose those big enough to matter and small enough to win. LISTEN to your people. If there is something they already see that is on your "list", that's a good place to begin.

NOTE: There are some expectations that can't wait… safety, treatment of children, laws. Beyond those, remember that the culture of your school is a particular way and *it got that way over time.* It will become the culture you seek *the same way.*

Developing expectations also takes clarity, and persistence, and support from the people who supervise you. If you are elevating expectations, you are going to ruffle some feathers. If the principal before you gave everyone high marks on evaluations and the board office wants you to use the  process to improve instruction, you'll need to have regular communications with your supervisor to remind them what *bringing change* can look like. Changing culture and raising expectations is bound to bring discomfort. A great practice is regular conversations with your immediate supervisor on your process so you can be on the front of the narrative.

Let's make the culture better. Here's the key: bringing your people together and lead them into *choosing* the expectations that lead to success. It's not just for student success… *choice and voice* are key elements of changing the culture of your faculty.

What if you're in a hurry? Can you force norms on people? Sure! You're their immediate supervisor. You can tell them what you want done and what happens if they don't do it.

There are consequences for doing it this way though. You have to follow up with non-compliance consistently and that can lead to diminished morale. If you are choosing the behavior (the norm, the expectations) against the will of your people, do know that they may only exhibit the behavior as long as you're there to make them. Again, there are some things that are important enough for you to make this choice (you'll have to decide what they are) but if you try to manicure everyone and everything at your school without the consent and engagement of the people you're working with, you'll get very tired, very quickly.

Even with a more strategic development of norms, you're going to expend a lot of energy. Bringing about change is critical. It's also exhausting so don't start it if you don't mean it. If your people think you don't have the oomph to stick with something through the hard parts, they'll always think you'll give in. Plan your path before you start moving. Choose norms that will lead to a better culture and are relatively hard for others to argue with. At one school I led, I chose *"please don't yell at students."* Simple, pretty easy to get people on board with, easy to teach. And, *you can't imagine how much good it does.*

Creating a new norm means you're constantly refining what it means… and doesn't mean to the people in your school. For example, *don't yell at students* means don't yell at the students in your class. It *also* means don't stand at the end of the hall and yell indiscriminately, *get to class!* Because that's… yelling at students. Talking to the teacher who is yelling at class change but thinks he's doing what you want him to do is part of the norm-setting process. Yes, we want students to get to class. No, we don't want to yell at them.

Your conversation goes to questions. What would work better than yelling and get us both things we want? How about a "one-minute until" bell? That way everyone hears a unique sound and knows it's time to get going. What about learning students' names that we don't teach? The same students come down the hall each day... what if we get to know their names and then we can ask them... one-on-one... how's it going? Relationships begin with names and change behaviors. It's not magic, but it's pretty close.

Over time, more and more of our people chose the norm we requested and others began to jump on board as they saw the potential of other ways to affect student behavior. We made what was an idea into an expectation... and yelling at students became the exception to our norms.

If you're thinking, wow, that was a really long process just to get teachers to do something they ought to do anyway... you're right. But if you make impactful choices about your norms, they can have a positive impact when they become a part of your culture. Guess what happened when we made courteous conversations with students a part of our culture? Student behavior toward teachers was improved.

What I see as a consistent problem in building culture... creating expectations is *too much* and *too fast*. I know you've read this before in this book, but your job isn't about making someone do or not do something; it's about influencing them in such a way that *they* make that choice, again and again, and make it without you being around to watch them do it.

Culture building requires great resolve on your part and the part of your administrative team. Don't say it if you don't mean it. Choose expectations that you can whole-heartedly support, teach, and enforce when necessary.

Does this get *everyone* on board? Normal distribution tells us that we'll *always* have outliers and exceptions. Culture is rarely unanimous; but pervasive can win the day.

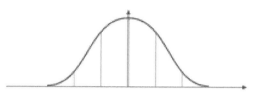

Normal distribution puts 16% of behaviors on each end with 68% in the middle. That would seem to suggest that if you get over 80% to accept the norm as an expectation, you have nearly everybody you mathematically should hope to get.
This is what I've noticed in practice: you don't even need that many to create a culture. Around 65-75% of your people, coalesced around a set of values and priorities is enough to have an exceptional school. Those in the 25-35%, find it harder to be the influencers they once were. They are most likely to acquiesce or relocate.

When you have enough people choosing higher expectations, you'll begin to attract more people like them. When you have a lot of people working at your school with low expectations and norms, they too will attract people like them.

Ask your teachers this: *would an excellent teacher of the year from another school visit our school and say, I want to work there? Why, or why not?*

Purpose. Vision. A great place to work. Collaboration. Respect. Teachers will drive past other schools to get to that. High expectations raised over time is the way that schools can be places of opportunity for students and meaningful workplaces for teachers.

194

GROWTH

As the principal or assistant principal, you are the pacesetter. You set the tone for your teachers and staff who in turn spread *your* attitude to the students.

Here's something that is often a defining attribute of a school:

How is failure viewed at your school?

Accountability systems for schools have recently been revised to feature, at least in part, growth models. Growth is about progress; failure is a necessary step towards progress; perfection, or at least the insistence on perfection as the metric, is an enemy of progress.

How you answer that essential question, (*How is failure viewed at your school?)* has implications in many areas. Here are three:

1. Assessment/Grading: If you are truly focused on progress and growth, you acknowledge that students don't begin their learning as experts. That understanding leads to a constructive approach towards learning. If you're there in your approach to school, you have to begin to explore what grades really mean and if you are assessing progress for growth or grading students for compliance. There's a big difference. If our ultimate goal is for students to master the standards, is it essential they all do so on the same days? We know that if learning is constant, then time has to be variable. Instead, we traditionally operate schools in reverse, where we hold time constant. If we don't recognize within that approach that learning will be variable, perhaps we are the ones who need schooling! Grading should be aligned to learning by assessing mastery

of application of standards and reporting progress and completion. Big topic, more another time, but fundamentally woven into the attitude your school has regarding the place of failure.

2. Innovation: Innovative schools regard failure as an important and expected step towards excellence. Curiosity is encouraged, fear of failing is discouraged. Everywhere I visit speaks of innovation, but compliance cultures are rare to truly innovate, and an uptight, fearful culture doesn't breed creativity. Our nature is to avoid being wrong and being called down; teachers and students alike often refrain from trying something new if they believe that the risk of reprisals is too high if it doesn't work at first. If you want to be a school of innovation, your people, from top to bottom, have to know that it's okay to work through the kinks to get something right, that they are encouraged to take the time to get it right.

3. Stress: Here's something our data is telling us, about schools all across the nation: there is more stress than ever before. Students are more stressed; teachers are more stressed; administrators can't show it, but they're stressed too! Part of this stress may be from outside sources and inherent to the job at hand, but some of the stress we're dealing with has come from our attitude about our work. We are learning organizations; we need to stress the process, not process the stress! If we adhere to the learning process, which is based on valuing people and meeting their individual needs, we will find ourselves more willing to focus on growth over time. I know that everyone faces statewide testing programs that create a deadline that makes teachers, students, and administrators feel like we have to be in a hurry. The *problem* with that approach is that being in a hurry doesn't work for everybody and more often generates stress that impedes progress. If we can take a healthy approach to failure, understanding its role in

growth and progress, we can skip the stress and drama and what comes with it and move forward on our journey to success.

Please don't misread the notion of embracing failure with one of lower expectations. This is of no value either. One of your primary jobs as the leader of a school is to help get and keep things in balance. Balancing the need for adequate time for learning with the goal of growth, progress, and excellence is a learning opportunity for you and an area in which you can lead your school to success. Just don't expect to get it perfect from the beginning.

One of the leaders in our session yesterday shared a powerful strategy her school has recently employed.

Instead of beginning their meetings sharing their successes, they instead share their failures.

Their approach is sure to lead to improved outcomes and a better place to work. The "perfect" business is exhausting! In schools, we can be slow to innovate because of our reluctance to try things we aren't already good at, aren't sure how to do, or are out of our comfort zone.

This isn't just a subtle difference in approach or a minor attitudinal difference. The "fear of failure" can be an overwhelming force that slows down growth, innovation and achievement. In short, our obsession with never being wrong can lead to us falling short of getting things right at all.

The children and adolescents growing up in our schools are citizens of a world that hardly any of their teachers experienced during their formative years. The world has changed, the accessibility to information has changed, and the speed and volume of information is head-spinning. Yet, some of our teachers haven't changed, or not nearly enough. While there are many reasons for their reticence, it's likely that the fear of failing is one of them, and the school's culture is an accomplice in keeping that fear alive. The challenge within that is the school's culture runs through those same teachers!

So, here you arrive. Captain Innovation. The Fountain of Ideas. The Change Leader. The people who brought you on board to lead the school want you to be innovative, but until you can change the culture about failure, your progress will be measured.

Changing your school's culture is all about changing the way that the adults who work there think. Before you are able to do that, you need to change the way that they feel, and that's climate. You need a climate that supports experimentation, trying new things, and a joy in the process before you can have a culture of innovation.

What do you do as the leader to produce such a climate? Here are some other ideas that might help you in your quest for a respect for failure and its ability to teach all of us:

- <u>Clarify your beliefs about learning</u>. While most everyone believes that learning comes from experience and through a process, at schools we place a high value on "perfection" and we can give mixed signals about what really matters. Our grading systems can be an example of that. Unfortunately, the emphasis can be on the grade and not the learning behind the grade. If you take a stab at aligning grades with learning (mastery, anyone?) you will make failure a more valued thing.
- <u>Honor and recognize the experimenters.</u> As long as we put the people who make a 97 on a test of recall on the highest step on the medal stand, we are devaluing the students (and their teachers) who may have learned the most and done the best work. It probably isn't the right time to *ignore* the folks who make all As (and it probably isn't the right thing

to do either) but what you *can* do is recognize those who are learning through experimentation. The scientists; the risk-takers; the innovators. Don't forget that achievement comes in lots of different packages. If you really want to innovate, you have to acknowledge the process, including the failing, that leads to discovery.

- Guarantee safety for those willing to be vulnerable. The quickest way to shut down innovation for a long time is to punish those who try new ideas that don't work on the first run. If you indeed are going to ask (push?) teachers to try new things, be innovative, do something new, you are going to need to have a safe place for them to land if it doesn't work.

- Share your own experience. Learning rarely happens in the absence of vulnerability. To really embrace the space of learning, you have to admit that, regarding the subject at hand, you don't know. It's much easier to talk about what we *do* know, and to put "what we don't know" in a basket of things that are out of reach. That attitude (perfect in what I know and perfectly happy to stop there) prevents learning. You have to try new things, and to get your faculty to do that, you have to get out on the limb, talk about your failures, and be willing to be seen as less than perfect. If you can do that, you are on your way to changing perspectives about learning... and failing.

- Raise the value of persistence. Persistence is the pathway to understanding failure and embracing the possibilities of learning. If you are going to move out of the "perfect business" into one where failure is embraced, be prepared for some pushback. The pushback will come when things don't work smoothly from the beginning. That's where we lose the people with the least amount of commitment to growth, which means you have to intercede with a message of persistence.

YES OR NO

Your school is either a fountain or a drain. It's either a place where ideas are appreciated, encouraged, and valued or a place where people learn to keep their ideas to themselves. So much of the climate for ideas, or lack of one, begins with the principal and administration.

Ideas are incredible, and they are literally everywhere around your school this very minute. The problem with a lot of those ideas is this: their owners aren't going to share them with you.

Your school is either a fountain or a drain. It's either a place where ideas are appreciated, encouraged, and valued or a place where people learn to keep their ideas to themselves. So much of the climate for ideas, or lack of one, begins with the principal and administration.

What do you do when someone has an idea? Do you make things easier for them or more difficult? Are you an idea accelerator or are you the brakes?

I know that you are called upon to be the leader of a safe, orderly school. That is important and shouldn't be taken for granted or lightly. Orderly can be good if used in the right measure. Order is easier to administer than freedom, and that's why most schools lean towards a more structured, policy-driven model of administration. The problem is this: if you lean too far in that direction, you'll end up with a place where the rules outweigh the ideas. If it's hard to get permission to move forward with an idea, the ideas will stop showing up. The converse is true as well; if ideas are welcomed, you'll have more and more of them.

Teachers, students, and staff have great ideas and innovations just waiting to be heard. At Morgan County High School where I was principal, we were having our annual "Club Fair" for our organizations to showcase who they are, what they do, and solicit members. One of our people had a great idea: let's do it outside and set it up with tables, music, food much like a festival.

That idea turned out to be a great one; the students enjoyed being outside, it was during our lunch periods so the clubs had a great turnout at their booths, and everyone had a chance to be creative in showing their wares.

While at this inaugural Club Fair, a student started talking to me. I asked him what he thought about the Club Fair and he said that it was good. He said that it was so good that we ought to do it every week! I asked him "what would that look like?" He said, "we don't need to advertise clubs every week, but we could have bands. Students who play guitar and sing can do it out here. And we can have a snow cone booth. And it'll be awesome."

From that conversation was born a tradition at our school. "Friday Alive," a mostly-weekly (weather-dependent on whether it was weekly) celebration of creativity, fun, and student talent. Friday Alive was a place for student performers to share their work; we had poetry jams; the marching band was a guest performer; the step team; the cheerleaders; even our versions of "The Voice" and on occasion Karaoke Friday. Friday Alive was, as the student described it to me to begin with, awesome.

That idea probably never rises up without a climate and culture where ideas matter. Here are a few reminders to the principal and assistant principal about making your school an idea factory:

- <u>Make it easier to get to 'yes' than to get to 'no'.</u> This one is straight-forward and plain. If the school's administration is always going to say 'no', you can expect that people will stop asking. If you're someone who will listen and try to figure out how it can happen rather than how it might go wrong, then you'll have more ideas than you've ever had. It *really* does begin with you.
- <u>Support other's ideas without becoming their new owner.</u> When students and teachers came to me with ideas, I worked to get to yes. That didn't mean that I became the person to carry out their idea. My questions were always ***"what will that look like?"*** and ***"how can I support you in your idea?"***
- <u>Make your school a laboratory for learning.</u> Don't squash an idea just because it may not work. Sometimes the best ideas need a few runs before they fly. (See "The Wright Brothers" and "Thomas Edison")

<u>As the principal, you are in a privileged position.</u> You literally have a creative team filling the classrooms around you. You can do awesome things at your school if you embrace the idea and idea maker. Whenever you hear those words, "I have an idea," be ready to be what they need to make those ideas reality.

EMPHASIS

*When you're the leader,
what you emphasize gets noticed.
What are you emphasizing at your school?*

As the leader of the school, what do you do on a regular basis to bring everyone's attention to the positive things that are going on at your school every day?

Here's a simple, yet impactful idea for your consideration.

At Morgan County High School, we are proud to be the Bulldogs! While I was principal there for nine years, one of our goals was to highlight the good, so we began to highlight those who did the right thing each Friday on our school's televised announcements.

Each Friday, we announced the weekly winner of the "Good Dog Deed" Award. There was a simple process to nominate someone-- we had a brief form asking who you were, who you were nominating and why. The criteria was equally simple-- we wanted to recognize those who had exemplified what it means to be a "good dog." Someone who had done you a kindness with no expectation of anything in return; someone who had gone above and beyond expectations; someone who had on a regular basis demonstrated respect and kindness to others on a regular basis.

At the end of the announcements each week, we dramatically announced the week's winner, sharing with the school who had nominated them, why they had done so, and then reminding them that each winner would receive an exclusive "Good Dog Deed" key chain as well as five coupons for five wings or tenders each from Zaxby's chicken. (A very big thing in the high school world!)

Additionally, the recipients were photographed that morning and added to the "Wall of Fame," the big board of people who had done great things that was located at the front door of the school. To get on the Wall of Fame, you had to make All-State Chorus, All-Region Basketball, have your artwork recognized in a juried show, or, be the good dog deed winner.

When you recognize as a school that you value how students treat others as much as you value other accomplishments, you have gone a long way towards setting a high standard of personal behavior.

Here's something that was interesting about the GDD Program, which we did for years every Friday: many of the recipients were also people who made nominations. When you are doing good, you are more likely to see good; when you are more likely to see good, you are more likely to do good as well.

There was a lot of fun in doing this over the years. I'd see some of my students in the parking lot at the grocery store, and they would shout over, "Hey, Doc! I'm pushing this cart back to the store for them! That's a good dog deed, right?" I developed a standard comeback for that one... "Yes! We want all of our students to be good dogs!"

When you're the leader, what you emphasize gets noticed. What are you emphasizing at your school?

Part VIII. Collaboration

TEACHERS WORKING TOGETHER

 *If school leaders want teachers to work together well as teams, they should invest the time to teach them to do so.*

Teamwork makes the dream work. TEAM: Together Everyone Achieves More. There is no 'I' in 'TEAM.'

All of these are true. All of these are great! And all of these are only a beginning to getting teams right in our schools. Sometimes as leaders, we know to our core that when our teachers work together we have better results, but we don't invest the time to help them learn how to work together.

Yes, we all want our faculty and staff to work well together in a number of different teams, small and large, criss-crossing each other and covering the needs of all of the students and parents of the school. We know that when we can get it right, teamwork will, as the saying goes, make the dream work!

Here's the problem: some of the teachers at any given school aren't great at working in teams. (Instances vary from school to school.) Sometimes even those teams that *appear* to be working together aren't always what they seem to be.

To a degree, many teachers find working as a team to be a bit unnatural. What they find natural is to be in charge of their own room, their own students, their own curriculum, and their own results. The truth is, many of the teachers who feel this way actually *do* deliver good results. What do you as the leader say then?

Many faculty members, depending upon the school, are the opposite. They gravitate towards working in a unit, dedicated to a cause, knee-deep in the data, and focused on the goals. Even those individuals only work well with others when the "others" are the right ones. I've visited many schools where grade level, department, or special interest teams have lots of good teachers but come together and create a deficit, not a strength.

If school leaders want teachers to work together well as teams, they should invest the time to help them do so.

This is hardly rocket surgery :-) but nevertheless, there are many leaders who are using hope as their best strategy for their teachers working together. They've put them together, assumed that they'll figure it out, and despite attending meetings with the team regularly *they have yet to establish how it works when the administrator isn't in the room.*

The goals that a school administrator has for her teams should be framed on what they do when you *aren't* around. Yes, you'll need to spend some time when you **are** around for a while to shape, model, and norm, but the goal should be to develop *fully functioning teams of teachers who improve instruction through their collaborative work and professional learning.*

To assume that all it takes for teams to work is an invitation to meet, a location, and a commonality among members (same department, same grade level) is wishful thinking at best. Working together as a team is like any other relationship. It takes time, it takes work, and it isn't always sunshine and cotton candy. You know right now the difference between effective and less-than-effective teams of teachers. If pressed to do so, you could name your most and least effective teams pretty quickly.

COLLABORATION

It is literally true that you can succeed best and quickest by helping others to succeed.

~Napoleon Hill

If you're doing teaching right, you're doing it with others. Teaching was once an individual endeavor, but we've learned how more effective we can be when we work together.

Some teams of teachers, however, are more effective than others. You know that from your work as a school leader. Do you know what makes one more effective than another? Let's take a look and perhaps it can help inform your work as you seek to design more effective teams.

Three Elements of Effective Teacher Teams

1. **Purpose**: The reason for bringing teachers together is to improve instruction. It's easier to improve your work if you're a part of a larger effort with others. Being a part of the team puts you in a culture of reflection, preparation, and continual improvement. When teachers come together without clarity of purpose, they often struggle. It's a good thing to have the purpose clearly stated and visible to maintain the focus. When it works, everyone knows the purpose of coming together and they are energized by it.

2. **Selflessness:** If each member of the team is committed to serving the interests of everyone else before their own, the team will be exceptionally successful. When a group of

teachers come together committed to the school's goals, to the success of all of the students, and to seeing their colleagues do well, everyone prospers. Since selflessness is not the default state for humankind, this can require some work. It's well worth the work, though. It's true that there's no 'I' in team, both literally and figuratively. When the individuals work for the team, the team also works for the individuals.

3. **Professionalism:** As the leader, if you want to have teams of teachers who work well, make sure to include an emphasis on professionalism. When educators (or any profession for that matter) behave in accordance to the highest standards for people in their field, you can begin your work with high expectations. Professionalism guides the behavior of individuals when no one is observing, watching, or inspecting. If the school's leaders can build a consistent culture of professionalism, they won't have to spend nearly as much time checking up on what their teachers are doing. We are counting on our teachers to behave in a professional manner even when we aren't there.

There are more than three elements of highly effective teacher teams, but if you get these right, you will be off to a good start. I've seen the best of teacher teams... and I've seen those who need a makeover.

That "makeover" is most likely to come from a source outside the team... you, the school leader. If you're deliberating on how to make one or more of your teams effective, consider these elements-- purpose, selflessness, and professionalism. Spend time with all of your teachers or just one team at a time. Once you have results, it's an easier path to understanding.

TEACHER TEAMS

Why do some teams of teachers work together well and others don't?

Teams of teachers can do amazing things together. Sometimes, however, they don't.

In my work supporting leaders in schools, "teams gone wild" is a frequent situation that I'm often asked about by principals and assistant principals. So the question at hand is , "why do some teams work well while others don't?" Here are some things to consider as you evaluate the efficacy of your teams.

Why Is My Teacher Team Not Working Well?

1. **The Leader.** Pardon the obvious irony here, but this is always the first place to look if things aren't going well. :-) (We are here for the truth! Don't be offended). If the team isn't functioning as it ought to be, is that a function of the team's leadership? In yesterday's column, we looked at seven things that principals can do to help teacher-leaders lead effectively. Often, if you can review the process of how your T-L is leading the team, you might find possible solutions. It could be in the style in which your T-L is directing the action. Remember, this isn't about blame or fault, but it is about developing practical solutions.

2. **The Team.** It might be the team. Sometimes teams (teams in general as well as teacher teams) just aren't a good mix. As the principal of the school, it's important to

think of the composition of your teams. Will the team members collectively be greater together than they are individually? Are the team members a good combination that will work together? As you plan your assignments for each school year, it's important to think about whether your team members will gel or not. There are a variety of personality trait quizzes that you can use to get a feel for who your teachers really are (if you don't know already). One of the best ways to have a highly functioning team is to **begin with** a team whose members complement one another. If it *is* the team, then you may have to take a more active role to shape their destiny for the remainder of the year until such time you can change assignments.

3. **The Obstinate One.** Ancient proverb: ***"One bad apple spoils the barrel."*** (Not sure how we got our bananas and bunches mixed in with apples and barrels, but "apple.. and... barrel" is the official verbiage.) That said, sometimes the team's issues aren't the leader, and not the team as a whole, but they're that one person. It's interesting to look at your faculty members and think about what other roles they can play. You have some teachers who would be great anywhere... and you have some that can mess up the dynamics on most any team. They may be a good classroom teacher individually (some of the people playing these roles are) but they don't get along well with colleagues. It establishes their authority with the team and allows them to build the relationship. If that doesn't work, you have to get involved and do what's necessary to get them on board.

4. **Hayfields and McCoys.** Sometimes a team doesn't work well and its not the leader, not the team, and not even the roadblock person. It's a turf war going on. Sometimes it's

two people; sometimes sides are drawn and nearly everyone is at odds. I always am interested when I ask teachers about their school and they tell me "we're like a family here!" That can be good, but sometimes... it can mean they're like a family. If you can drive your folks back into the notion of being a **team of professionals**, you may be able to recapture their mental model of what they're doing. However, if feuds are more than temporary, they can shut down the success of the team. It's worth monitoring.

5. **You.** It's been my experience that teachers and students will focus on and do well in areas that are established as important to the school. You need for teachers to be able to work together without you there all of the time (it's just impossible for you to be everywhere all of the time and you need to build capacity). What you **must** do is maintain appreciation, support, and attention to their efforts as a team. Recognize what people do in teams and they'll do it well. Assign them, give them a T-L and forget about them? That's the recipe for non-functioning teams. You have a lot of influence on whether teams will work well or not. They have to go through the learning process together on how to be a good team. If you fly in on your magic carpet and fix everything all of the time, that may lead to learned helplessness rather than the capacity to lead that it's supposed to get to. Always measure your response.

LEADERSHIP TEAMS

What is that you want to accomplish by bringing a group of teachers together and calling them "the leadership team" or something similar?

Here's a question for you if you're a principal : **what is the purpose of your "leadership" team?**

What is that you want to accomplish by bringing a group of teachers together and calling them "the leadership team" or something similar?   Have you pondered that question or are you having a leadership team because there was one when you got there?

It's reasonable to suggest that a *leadership team* might serve several purposes depending upon what you've charged them to do. <u>The purpose of your leadership team should precede picking your teachers, but in many cases it doesn't.</u>   So, what is your leadership team about? Why do you bring them together?

Here are a few purposes of school-level leadership teams. Think about which best describes yours.

1. **Administration**: This remains one of the functions of many grade-level and department leaders in schools around the country. In these configurations, the leadership team is responsible for completing purchase orders, distributing materials, and for the most part serving as a distribution center for the members of her department or team.

2. **Representative:** Some leadership teams are set up like a *faculty senate* or a *student council.* The members of the team represent a group; they come together and listen to a variety of things on an agenda. They may give their opinions, and in some schools they even 'vote' on items. This representative function looks different than a purely administrative design; the teachers represent their colleagues and come to your leadership team meeting to interact with the information and make decisions.

3. **Ambassador:** This is the reverse of the *representative* form of leadership team. In this format, you bring teachers in and prepare them to represent *the leadership team* with their grade-level or department.

4. **Hybrid:** Many schools have a hybrid of the previously-mentioned leadership teams. They do some of the administration work, and some representing of their teachers, and some representing *to* their teachers.

5. **Distributed:** In this model, you distribute the leadership of the school to a number of people. Some may be *department heads* or *grade-level leaders*, others might be responsible for a program or initiative (PBIS, Freshman Academy, Pre-K). This is different because you give broad authority to the individuals in charge of each group of teachers.

Which describes your leadership team? There isn't a right answer, but it's one that you should be intentional about. Obviously, some schools have a faculty who is ready for more responsibility than another. The same is true for leaders; some leaders are more apt to share responsibility than others.

What you might consider is this: what model of leadership team would best serve the school and the students?

Part IX. Mechanics

ORGANIZATION

As the principal, you DON'T need to be in charge of everything. But, you can be in charge of HOW everything works. With a process for events you can ensure a level of excellence in all that you do at your school.

When they hired you, they said they wanted an instructional leader, which they do. What they *also* want is someone who is good with relationships. And, by the way, you also will need to be a really good manager of the operation and be excellent in organization.

Yep… that's a lot! We can help you with the organization part. Begin with this… a binder with sheet protectors. I'm admittedly a techie and sure you can do this electronically, but some things just work better in analog.

Now, with the binder, the sheet protectors and the help of your administrative assistant, keep a sheet on "how to" do your school. Then as events happen, you engage in a process to ensure things run well. It's simple: Plan– Brief–Implement–Debrief.

The **planning** happens well before the event, giving yourself more time if the event is a bigger one. Most events you can plan a month out; graduation would require several months of planning.

Briefings happen around a week before the event and include all people who will be involved in the event. This is when everyone confirms that their part is taken care of and if need be a rescue plan can be launched.

The day comes for your event and you **implement** your plan. Then as soon as you can and no later than the next day, go straight into your **debrief** where you bring the same people back from the briefing and review the event and what changes need to be made for the next time you do it.

What do you put in the sheet protector and into the binder? The planning sheet, including notes from the debrief. Then when it's time to do this again *next year*, you'll have the instructions… what to do, when to do it, from the previous version.

As the principal, you DON'T need to be in charge of everything. But, you can be in charge of HOW everything works. With a process for events (especially the debrief and the book) you can ensure a level of excellence in all that you do at your school.

It's a great way to teach norms and to set the bar for *how we do things* around here. If you're thinking that people get tired of all these meetings, think again. Having *clarity* on what's going on instead of doing things at the last minute (which you basically eliminate with the process) is music to the ears of the organizing people at your school.

 Your custodians love it as they now are in the loop on everything happening at your school. And, your briefings and debriefings can be done as stand-up meetings.

(When you have a stand-up meeting, you can count on it going faster. People are having to stand so they are more likely to keep it moving. Also, when they don't *get settled* into a seat, they are more engaged in the briefing and it goes faster.)

A Standard of Excellence

When we bring people into our schools, we have an opportunity to influence the way they think about us. Whether they think we've got it together... if they see us as professionals... what kind of organization we're running.

I cannot believe that principals accept some of the things I've seen at school events. For one, make sure you have a speaker and microphone that work and can be comfortably heard by the people who are in attendance. This is one of the things that was listed on the *resources* list for most of our events. We had two identical sets at all times (in addition to built-ins at the auditorium and gym). We were going to have a working system and a back up. Planning ahead solves a lot.

What is shared at your school has your autograph next to it when you're the principal, so don't share things that look bad. I've been to events where the program had been copied so crooked it looked like the Leaning Tower of Pisa. Plan-Brief-Implement-Debrief takes care of those problems, typically upfront and always in the debrief.

When you have events, have programs so they can go in memory books. Have pressed tablecloths (the ones with your school logo on them... order more than one so you always have one clean)... have ferns. **Behavior is influenced by environment**... not just behavior at that moment but behavior in general and over time. Do things in a first-class manner and correct any missteps in the debrief.

HIRING SEASON

It's SO much better to take time and hire effectively than to suffer through poor choices in hiring. Those poor choices can hurt your students, your teachers, and others' perception of your judgment.

When it's hiring season, you need to be working with urgency. There are only so many candidates for the positions you may need, and you need to prioritize this work. It's complicated by the timing: hiring season comes when you're registering students and families for the next school year, preparing your school for end-of-the-year testing, and doing the daily, busy work of the school. Maybe that's why some leaders don't get the hiring season right--- the other priorities are too much and you aren't able to immerse yourself in hiring because of those other tasks at hand.

If that's you, here's something for you to consider: what you do during hiring season is a gift that keeps on giving. If you do well, it's a treasure; if you do poorly, it's a gag gift. You can put in the time and energy needed to do well in hiring, or you are at risk for spending much more time correcting your hiring mistakes and cleaning things up. **It's SO much better to take time and hire effectively than to suffer through poor choices in hiring.** Those poor choices can hurt your students, your teachers, and others' perception of your judgment.

So, if you have people to hire, put other things down. Read resumes, call references, host visits to your school. Either get busy hiring, or you'll be busy next fall wishing you'd done better on the front end.

Time well spent.

First and foremost, **make sure that you are connected at the hip to whomever works with you on Human Resources.** Each system has their own nuances about the hiring process and you need to follow the policies and protocols that your system has in place. Beyond that, those who invest more time into a task are more likely to be effective in completing it. Don't rest until you get your people in place, begin their transitional phase, and start to engage them in the culture of your school.

As we move forward, school leaders should expect to spend more time than ever in developing the talent in your building to grow effective teachers and a top-notch faculty. You make that job harder than it might have to be if you do poorly in hiring. The time you spend now is invested into getting teachers and staff that will make a positive impact at your school.

What to ask yourself before you begin interviewing candidates.

I get a lot of requests for "interview questions," but before we get to them here are questions *about* your interviewing process for you to ***answer*** rather than ask.

- Before you begin to conduct an interview, ask yourself, ***"what am I hoping to learn?"*** If you can enter the interview with **specific goals** and guide your questions accordingly, you'll get more from the time you're investing.
- As a part of the overall process, consider this question: ***"what do I want to learn about this candidate that I WON'T*** *discover in an interview?"* What you discover, even during the best of interview sessions, is LIMITED. How does an interview show you the skills and dispositions you're looking for in a candidate? What if someone isn't great in an interview session but is exceptional in a teaching situation? Again, when you're looking for

candidates, <u>stay focused on your goal</u>-- you are looking for good teachers. (Counselors, APs, etc...). You are NOT the judge of a "who can interview the best" contest. You are an investigator... a scientist... not a pageant judge.

- Finally, another question for your consideration: ***"how will I find out what I want to learn about this candidate?"*** Using the resources and time you have available, how might you learn what you want to know? The best way to know if someone can effectively teach isn't to ask them about it--- it's to watch them! If conditions allow, watch a candidate deliver a sample lesson at your school. Get others in their potential grade level or department to watch them with you. If that's not possible, you need to talk to others who have seen this candidate teach. *Having connections with administrators in other schools and systems* helps you have a conduit to find out what you want to know. You call a friend and find a friend of theirs, and you can discover many of the questions you'd like to have answered.

Try to calibrate your thinking into this: it's not interview season; it's HIRING season. Keep you focus on HIRING good teachers. The interview is just a part of it all... it's like the bread on your sandwich. It frames the rest of the things you do for hiring... checking references, reading resumes, watching your candidates teach sample lessons.

<u>*Questions you may want to use during an interview session.*</u>

Getting set to conduct interviews? Looking for some questions that might help you gain insight on your candidates?

Here are some that might lead to insights!

- We don't expect for you to be perfect, but we are counting on you to be coachable. Tell us a time when someone coached you, you listened, and you improved.

- Teamwork is important to us at our school. Tell us about a team that you were on that was successful. Why was it successful? What was your role on the team?
- Collaboration is a core value at our school. Please share with us your experience in collaborating with other teachers. What's been successful and what's been challenging when you've collaborated with others in your work?
- We intentionally are building a positive climate at our school. Teaching can be hard. How do you handle the stress without becoming negative? On a scale of 1 to 5, 5 being the most positive, how positive are you when things are tough?
- Partnering with parents of our students is a cornerstone of our school. Talk about your experience in positively connecting with parents. What will you pledge to the parents of your students when you meet them at the beginning of the school year?
- Who is someone at your school or work that has helped you become better at your work? What did they do and why was it helpful?
- Who is someone at your school or work that *you* have helped become better at your work? What did you do and why was it helpful?
- We are looking for teachers who can engage and challenge their students. What does that mean to you? What will your classroom look like when it's engaging and challenging?
- Tell us a story of how you worked with a student whose behavior was regularly non-compliant. How did you help them find success?
- We believe in growth at our school so we will be providing feedback for our teachers, just as we expect them to do so for their students. Tell us how you will respond to feedback on your performance?

ETHICS AND PROFESSIONALISM

What talks about gets done. If you have a presentation on ethics for an hour during preplanning and that's your strategy for building a culture of ethical behavior, it better be a really good presentation!

My friend Paul Shaw served as Director of the Ethics Division of the Professional Standards Commission here in Georgia and he and I delivered a number of sessions for school administrators. Our effort was to support our administrators in behaving ethically and professionally, but also developing a culture of ethical and professional behavior at their schools.

Dr. Shaw is a terrific presenter, cares about education, and is going to make you laugh even while discussing topics of such gravity.

One thing he shared at every session we did was this reminder to the administrators: *everyone is going to be watching you because you're entrusted with the two things they care the most about– their children and their money.*

As an administrator, you need to know that all eyes are on you. (Shoutout Tupac) And in the world we're in now, it's likely that you're being videoed or recorded.

On one hand this is easy… be where you're supposed to be and do what you're supposed to do.

A challenge for all leaders is this: the further you ascend in the hierarchy of an organization, the less likely it is that people around you will correct you. (Shoutout Hans Christian Andersen)

Everyone needs a "get-back coach," someone who pulls us back on the sidelines before we get a penalty. As you lead your school, try to avoid being detached from what got you there. Keep people around you who will not merely give you praise and confirmation, but will challenge you to be better each day.

Leading a culture of ethical behavior

What talks about gets done. If you have a presentation on ethics for an hour during preplanning and that's your strategy for building a culture of ethical behavior, it better be a *really* good presentation!

Unfortunately, that's often the case. I ask principals in my classes when they've had specific PD or conversations about ethics to the faculty at large, and it is typically only at the beginning of the year. Even those have been tempered by being delivered as modules online. I get it… we want to maximize time and that's certainly something you could do in a module, but… how you spend your time reveals your priorities.

I often ask principals… if something happened at your school that was a violation of the educator code of ethics… what would you do *then?* Whatever that is… do that up front and proactively.

Unfortunately, even with ongoing conversations about ethical behavior, some educators make bad choices. Dr. Shaw suggests that when the temptation is strong and the risk of being caught seems slim, people may act outside of their typical nature. The more we can do, Shaw suggests, to minimize space for unethical behavior, the better we reduce the potential.

For example, as the principal, you may want to develop policies (with your system, of course) regarding your employees texting with students. An easy way to avoid entering an unsafe space is to include a parent and someone from the school on the text threads. Yes, we want our teachers and coaches to develop positive and appropriate relationships with our students. Those relationships need boundaries and eliminating 1:1 text messaging would play a part in establishing firm boundaries.

Developing a strategy of professional learning throughout the year on ethical behavior raises the topic to everyone's consciousness and can be a strong reminder of the high standards all educators are required to live up to.

Professionalism Abides

We don't talk enough about professionalism to get the value from it that is always within our grasp. So much of your work as the principal deals with *behavior.* Student behavior, yes, but even moreso, *adult behavior.* Isn't it true that if all of your teachers and staff were exemplary in professionalism, their behaviors in all areas would be what you're after?

If their behaviors are *not* what you're after, why would you rate them as excellent in their performance reviews? (aka, observations and conferences) Most states and systems have professionalism as one of the standards for effective teaching used in teacher evaluation. If we have teachers doing some of the things I've been told they've done, why do they continue to get adequate scores in professionalism?

For clarity's sake, I think culture and influence have a stronger impact on staff behavior than carrots and sticks (evaluation scores), but if culture and influence fail to change the behavior, it's time to use another strategy.

Here's an example: a principal that I coach has a teacher who does well in the classroom but not with her grade-level team members. She checks all the boxes for the in-class behaviors– lesson planning, assessment, instructional strategies, differentiation. What she doesn't do well is get along with others, particularly the members of her team.

When they have PLC meetings, she sits away from everyone else, arms folded, often looking at her phone, completely disengaged. It has a negative effect on her teammates, one of whom is the team leader who does everything administration ever asks and then some, the other two being brand new teachers.

After conversations with the disengaged teacher, the principal hoped that there would be a change in these behaviors. There was not.

When the principal shared these things with me, my question was, *what is her most recent rating on Professionalism in the evaluation system?* In Georgia, we have a 1-4 rating system. My advice was to give her a 1 on professionalism. I would expect that would bring her to the office to have a conversation about the rating, which the principal could make into a conversation about professionalism.

Like so many concepts in the school world, *professionalism* requires definition over time. It is often easier to understand by observing what it is *not.* And like other things in the school, we make it important by talking about it, sharing a conceptual definition, and then clarifying it in real-time and in real life.

GET THINGS DONE

If you want your day as the principal to run well, the beginning is the most critical. Make a habit to greet your teachers as they arrive;see your students as they get to school as well. (drop-off line, bus lane, parking lot) Be a part of morning announcements: help establish the tone of the day.

It's the weekend, and you need to be enjoying yourself. Spending time with people you love doing things you love to do. Getting refreshed, refocused, and ready for another week of leading your school.

Are you instead spending some, most, or all of your weekend doing work?

Get out of that routine by better balancing your tasks **during the week.** Take your weekends back by being more effective during the week. Balance your time to effectively complete the tasks you need to accomplish so there won't be so many left to do when the weekend arrives.

Easier said than done? Perhaps, but there are some **strategic habits and attitudes** you can adopt that will help you to get your days more balanced.

1. **Seize the Morning to Seize the Day.** If you want your day as the principal to run well, the beginning is the most critical. If you can make a habit to greet your teachers as they are arriving; then see your students as they get to

227

school as well. (drop-off line, bus lane, parking lot) Be a part of morning announcements: help establish the tone of the day. Then, depending on the size of your school, make a sweep of as many classrooms as you can. If you're able to get to some of them, that's great; if your school is small enough where you can get to all of them, that's even better. Getting around to your students and teachers, just to check in and just to set tone can be the prevention that's worth a pound of care. The mornings are golden hours and if you can *get everyone off to a good start doing what they ought to be doing* you'll be amazed at how you can recapture control of your days.

2. **<u>One Thing At A Time</u>** After you establish the foundation of the day by being visible, it's time to work on the tasks at hand. Observations? Meetings with teachers? Planning? You have lots to do, but work to get things done before spreading yourself out to the next thing. If you can develop the habit of **working on things to their completion**, you'll be giving yourself time that you don't even know you've been giving away. The constant starts and restarts are a big part of the time loss that happens to you as the leader. When you do a classroom observation, don't take notes and go back later and complete the writeup on the platform; spend five more minutes at *that* time to get it completed. (And those who say you can't do that should at least give it a try!) The people who get tasks completed are the ones that are able to focus long enough on a particular thing to get it accomplished. You can do it; it's an attitude, and then it becomes a habit.

3. **<u>Your Emergency Is Not Necessarily My Emergency</u>** When principals and assistant principals tell me they spend all day every day putting out fires, I often mention that you might want to spend some more time in the fire prevention business then! Part of this is established in number one, above, by framing the day every day for the students and

teachers at your school. Another is by strategically training your faculty and staff in how to resolve many (most) of their issues without the need to bring them to the administration. There are some schools that have established the norm that everything is a crisis and the principal's job is to solve everyone's problems.

Those schools are consistently distracted from their real work (learning) and the principal and assistant principal are indeed always putting out fires. To get out of that business, **you need to clarify what your job as principal really is.** If the central office thinks you're an instructional leader (they do) and your faculty thinks you're a firefighter, you have a problem.

Clarify what you do, help prepare your faculty and staff to solve many of their problems and you'll all of a sudden have time you didn't know existed. This really works. You have to get it established in a way that makes it look like you aren't insensitive to their needs . (Being transparent is critical. Tell them WHY you are wanting to teach them new ways to handle classroom events. Metacognition. It really will work with time and commitment).

There are other things that you can do to help balance your daily work that we will discuss in future posts, but these are three to begin with that are high-impact strategies that will literally get you operating more effectively during the week so you can have your weekend back.

PROBLEM OR ANNOYANCE

Things happen at the school constantly and as the leader, you are called on to know what's mild (an inconvenience or an annoyance) and what's caliente (a real problem that needs immediate attention). The sooner you're able to distinguish between the heat levels of what happens at your school, the better you're able to lead and manage your building.

At your friendly neighborhood wing place, you have choices of how much heat you want on your food. Most wing spots have cool (hot?) names for their levels, including "burn your bottom", "sizzlin' or screamin'", to "lava, magma, insanity."

I'm amazed at how they keep these ingredients separated in the kitchen and how seldom it is that orders get accidentally swapped at the window. Our heroes of the hot wings keep it straight somehow, offering a range of choices for your culinary delights.

Your job as a school administrator can sometimes feel like the heat index. But in this context, you don't get to order what you want; instead you have to figure out which level you're getting.

Often, school leaders, particularly when they're new, can mistake a ghost pepper for a pimiento, much to their discomfort. Things happen at the school constantly and as the principal or assistant principal, you are called on to know what's mild (an inconvenience or an annoyance) and what's caliente (a real problem that needs immediate attention). The sooner you're able to distinguish between the heat levels of what happens at your school, the better you're able to lead and manage your building. However, your discernment likely will come from experience, and much of it will be from originally getting it wrong.

230

Problem or Annoyance?

My friend and colleague Eric Arena, Superintendent of the Putnam County School System in Eatonton, GA often says that "it's not a problem until it's a problem." There are things that fall into this category for certain. If you hire spouses to work at your school, it may work out fine. It's neither illegal, unethical, or inappropriate to do so. While it's going along well, it's not a problem. Then, let's say one of the spouses gets a bad rating on their evaluation. Afterwards, the other spouse decides they want to relinquish their role as coach, director, or sponsor because they want to support their spouse. That's a problem that wasn't one... until it was. Even more than circumstances in that category, there's a genuine question that I find new administrators asking themselves: is what I'm examining an annoyance or is it a problem? You can't handle nuisances in the same manner you handle real problems. Sometimes you can be bothered by something someone has done or is doing and it's a bother to you but not REALLY what you should consider as a problem.

So how do we decide if something IS a problem? Let's define it with examples:

- Your system has a policy on dress code for employees. Your people are only permitted to wear jeans on specifically designated days. You walk around the school on a day that's NOT one of those days and find a second grade teacher dressed in jeans. Privately, you bring her aside and ask her about what she's wearing. She tells you she didn't get a chance to do laundry and this was all she had clean today. Problem? Annoyance? And if it IS a problem, how do you address it?

- Speaking of faculty dress, you're principal of a school and you have a faculty member who graduated from your school's rival across town. He regularly wears jackets from that school (where he once worked and in whose attendance zone he still lives). Your system (unlike the one in the previous example) has a relatively loose dress code policy for employees. There's nothing in your policy that says employees can't wear jackets with insignias. Other employees regularly roll their eyes when they see him do this. Problem? Annoyance? And if it IS a problem, how do you address it?
- You're new as the principal at a middle school and you have inherited a school counselor who has been at the school for twenty years. His office looks like he hasn't thrown away anything during that entire time. To you, he seems to always be a little scattered. He either gets things done at the last minute or at the minute after that. You wonder if the work would be of a higher quality if he was better organized. Little things seem to be dropped regularly. You are concerned about correcting him because the teachers and community love him (he's survived some health scares over the years) and they are just getting to know you. Problem? Annoyance? And if it IS a problem, how do you address it?
- One of your teachers is a self-proclaimed "electronics curse." She says she can break the internet. So, she hasn't gotten on board with keeping her website updated. Some of the parents of her students are frustrated about grades not being posted and not getting replies from emails. Other parents love her and think she's the best thing this side of Dolly Parton. Problem? Annoyance? And if it IS a problem, how do you address it?

One person's jalapeno is another person's habanero.

In coaching hundreds and hundreds of school leaders, I've observed that some look at inconveniences as problems, while others have problems that they have not been able to distinguish as such. So what is a problem? It's relative. Take dress code, again. If your system has made a point of emphasis on employee dress, then it is truly a problem when those for whom you are accountable don't do follow the policy. There are other locations where it might not be as important. You need to know the lay of the land and what those who supervise YOU determine to be annoyances/problems.

Here are indicators that an action you're examining is indeed a problem:

1. **It impacts others.** Is it a problem when your seventh-grade teacher wears a shirt that says, "Sarcasm. It's How I Hug."? It might draw a laugh from you, but what does it do to influence the students that the teacher supports? How an action impacts others often can help you determine whether it's a problem. I think a teacher who raises her voice to children is a problem. How does it relate to your school's or system's culture? If it involves others, perhaps you should see it as a problem.
2. **It's against policy.** This is easy, and then it's not. When you begin to examine the actions of people at your school, you might find that a LOT of things are done (or not done) contrary to policy. It's why professionalism and ethical behavior are so important to the school's well-being. If you work somewhere where people cut corners on small things, eventually they will do so with big things too.
3. **It's a matter of safety.** If you have an electrical outlet that doesn't have a cover on it, is that a nuisance or a problem? If you have rooms where they fire bell or intercom doesn't

work: inconvenience, or problem? If there are floor waxers routinely in the hallways of the school that might otherwise block the movement of students and teachers... problem? Look, you have to build a team to examine the operation of your school because if it's only you, you'll be exhausted. Make safety a priority and then you'll have lots of eyes to evaluate preferences vs. problems. (We don't have Diet Coke in the drink machine... again. That's an inconvenience...bordering on... but a preference, not a problem. Door locks not working? Not a preference, it's a safety problem.)

4. **It will rise to another level.** If you have something that is going to move from school level to regional, system, or state level, then it's probably more than a nuisance. Don't be afraid to communicate with the people who supervise and support you. I know there's that feeling that "I don't want them to think I don't know what I'm doing", but I guarantee you there's a greater risk in under-communicating than over-communicating. Those at central office who have the experience you don't have should be able to help you determine a course of action that's commensurate with the situation. If you think it's going to end up at Central Office eventually, you should share it with them immediately.

5. **Your gut tells you so.** Don't discount your little voice. It's not always right, but it's your experience and insight activating for you in a time of need. Most of us are more regretful of NOT listening to our guts than in doing so.

WORKING WITH THE DISTRICT

The most effective way to advance in any organization is by having someone at the next level who is a champion for your work and an advocate for your advancement.

Who at the Board Office is a champion for you and your school? Who will be an advocate for you when your name comes up in conversation there? Who is the person who will speak up for your advancement in the system?

If you're a brand-new principal, you may read *advancement* and think *hold on now… I haven't processed **this** advancement yet… not ready to think about another one!* Sure, but, advancement isn't just a new position at another level. Advancement is also about ever-improving the narrative about you. Much of what people at the central office think about you comes from what other people say about you. If you have a champion… not a hype man, and not anything disingenuous.. someone who knows you, knows your work, and *gets* what you're doing, then you have something valuable and necessary.

Like any relationship, you need to invest time to keep it strong. ALWAYS know who your champion is, and in the other direction, think about whose champion are you. What do you do to advocate for others in your organization? Being a champion helps you understand the role of your champion and what you need from them.

235

Soundbites from Central

There are a few superintendents and area supervisors I know that, either by design of their system or by their priority, spend a lot of time at their schools and get to see for themselves how the school is operating and what the principal is doing. Just like in the classroom, a superintendent can come to your school and see your work by _observing the work of others._ They are able to see the results of your efforts in the actions of the people of the school.

There also are many superintendents who have very lean staff at Central Office and aren't able to get out to schools as often as they might like. So how do they know if you're doing a good job or not?

Soundbites. From people they know and trust who _have_ spent time at your school. Perhaps the Special Services Director... instructional support members... maintenance. They also hear what teachers, parents, and even students have to say about school. Sometimes they hear what they have to say about you too. It's fair game... you are in a results-driven environment.

What I have found to be good advice is this: meet regularly with your immediate supervisor. In some small systems, that may mean the Superintendent while in others it may be a coordinator or director. Whomever it may be, developing and nurturing _an ongoing conversation_ about your school and what you're doing there is beneficial for you. While people may be able to visit your school and see _what_ is happening, it may take speaking with you to understand _why_ and to know how it's going and what's next. THAT'S what you talk about in these ongoing conversations. You're not trying to hype yourself... you're merely developing a more informed narrative about what is happening at your school, adding in information that has to come from that level.

236

Remember this, please. Everyone is making their assessment of you based on results, judgment, and how you treat people. I've always thought I had more control on the latter of those so I tried to make sure I had it in the bag in case I messed up on the first two.

Queen here; middle-management there

Among many other wonderful things about being a principal, one is this: you're as close to being a queen or king than you most likely will ever get.

Yes! You can get things happening when you're the principal... typically you have a lot of space in which to make decisions, do things, and that's a royal place to be.

When you're the principal, you're a celebrity! People know who you are (and often want to talk to you in the produce section of your local grocer... pro tip- go at 10:00 PM)! When you are in your school and you walk up on a group of teachers talking, they immediately stop when they see you... you know... out of respect. ;-)

All kidding aside, when you're at school you are in charge.

Then you go downtown for the principals' meeting. Please leave the tiara in your car. You are now middle-management.

Being middle-management is hard, but it's even harder when you are used to being the king. You'll need to embrace it though.

And there, you remember you serve as the principal of the school, but also as a *member of the District Leadership Team.* In that role, you widen your gaze to look at an even bigger picture than the one you see every day.

PARTNER WITH PARENTS

Decades of social science research have demonstrated that differences in quality of schools can explain about one-third of the variation in student achievement. But the other two-thirds is attributable to non-school factors.

Richard Rothstein, 2010, How To Fix Our Schools

Working to lead students to success without developing a partnership with their parents is like driving a car with a flat tire. Cross country in the rain. Without windshield wipers.

You get it. Research tells us that the influence of parents, or others raising a child in place of parents, is among the most impactful in determining student achievement. We know that a particular type of parental involvement is very effective in leading to student achievement, but at schools we typically don't spend much time to foster that behavior.

John Hattie's meta-analyses show a high effect size for parental involvement* (.58). There are ***other*** things that are prominent at schools everywhere that ***don't*** have the same research basis, but we do them anyway. For example, homework (.29 effect size); 1:1 technology (.16) and mentoring (.12). (Remember that anything below a .40 effect size is not considered to be successful in advancing student achievement.)

So, it's possible that we do things that may not yield a lot for our efforts while missing out on something that could make a great difference. Why? We know that we tend to do things the way they've always been done. Even when we make an effort to "increase parental involvement," we often spend time on things that don't necessarily produce a high yield.

Let's look at Hattie's study of different types of parental involvement (2018) and their effect on student achievement.

Supervising Child's Homework	0.19
Parent Participation in School Activities	0.14
Communication with School and Teachers	0.14
Parent Listening to Child Reading	**0.51**
*High Expectations for Student Achievement	**0.58**

(and verbalizing these to the child)

According to Hattie, more than homework, more than 1:1 technology, more than mentoring, more than getting parents to come to school events, more than communication between teachers and parents, what really makes the biggest difference *is when parents establish and communicate high expectations for student achievement with their child.*

It would seem to reason that we the school would work *really hard* to encourage and influence parents in communicating these high expectations. Yet, when I talk about school separately to parents and teachers/administrators, there is often frustration on each part with the other. Rather than dissect those arguments, perhaps we the school would benefit in our mission by seeking more positive relationships with parents.

If we could become partners with parents (and often we do!), we can more intentionally focus on a tidal shift of educational expectations among the families of our school. To become partners, we first have to have a relationship, which follows making connections with each other. Those relationships lead to trust, and with trust influence, particularly if we never grow tired of working to earn that trust.

HOW to build partnerships with parents.

Mindset. Within the school, administrators, faculty and staff who genuinely respect and value parents are more likely to connect, develop a relationship, and establish a partnership. Like all relationships, it takes work, but we are well-served if we reach out an open hand (and an open heart) to the parents of our students. Our actions, whatever they may be, may influence how parents react.

Reimagined Interactions. Spring-boarding from a positive mindset about parents, we need to reimagine what our relationships with parents look like. When we bring them to campus, what if we thought of them as parents of highly-prized college recruits? What would that look like at your school? What if you examined your model of the "parent-teacher conference"? What might you do to make it more of a meeting of partners in an important joint effort? Our interactions with parents begin on the phone and at the front door. What is your standard for those interactions? What do we say about our attitude about parents with each call and visit to the front office?

What KIND of Parental Involvement? While we often talk about parental involvement, what exactly is it and how do we measure it? According to the Harvard Family Project (2005), *parental involvement is associated with higher student achievement outcomes*. What involvement? **Parents reading with their children** is the most important. As children grow older, it is their **parents expectations** about school that most impact their approach to learning. While at school we have often measured our parental involvement with attendance at evening events, volunteer hours, and papers signed and delivered on time, the real impact on student performance comes from parents reading with their children and having conversations about school.

AND EVERYTHING ELSE

...Other duties as assigned...

This book was never meant to be everything a principal would ever need to know. It would be significantly heavier if that were the case, and I'm quite sure that neither me nor anyone else could prepare such a text.

I do want to acknowledge that we haven't covered everything... someone will pick this up (thanks for that!) and wonder why we didn't have a chapter on *this* or *that*.

You may even say, *hey you didn't cover _____ at all, but you talked about balance and perfectionism and priorities in fifteen different chapters.*

To that I would say... you are correct. Remember this book is built from thousands of visits to school leaders and some things come up in multiple topics. They are the threads that tie together various parts of the principal experience.

This book is to support new or newer principals and to prepare future ones so *choices were made* which is yet another recurring theme. As we're finishing up, there are a handful of items that I'd like to briefly mention here:

- <u>*Learning.*</u> You. The Principal... please keep learning. And not just about leadership or spreadsheets or motivation, but *be the learner that you'd like your people to be.* It keeps you grounded in what's going on around you and is very healthy for your brain. My $0.02 worth is to find something interesting to you but not related to your job. What it will reveal to you are things that will help you in your job… like the essential pieces of learning (curiosity and vulnerability). So when you take up something that you are interested in and you already know you aren't an expert (not yet a novice!) it opens your eyes in ways you often struggle in when you're only engaged in *what you know at some level.* I'm currently practicing pencil sketching, watching a lot of videos about physics, and reading about neuroscience. (I'm below basic in all of them but very interested!)

- *Network.* Similar to attorneys and MDs, you are in practice. Your work isn't a discrete set of actions, but one that requires your inquiry, assessment, and judgment. While you gain your own experience, you can leverage that of others by engaging in a network of other principals. You get better at your job by talking to those who are also doing it. It's valuable to have networks in and outside your system. And, it helps you feel less alone.

- *Feedback.* To be an effective coach and leader, you should work on delivering feedback in a positive and productive manner. I know there are books about "courageous" conversations. Giving feedback is just your job. If you can't do it, you are in the wrong business. Make connections, build relationships, earn trust, but don't stop there. You do those things so you can help them grow, so you can influence what they do. If you had a daughter who was good at softball and you paid a hitting coach to work with her each week, would you be okay if she never told your daughter what she was doing wrong? If she was afraid she'd hurt your daughter's feelings? No! If she did those things you would find a different coach. I'm not suggesting you (or that coach) be cruel or abusive... I AM saying that you have to tell people the truth and help them get better from it. Poon Lim was a Chinese sailor who was on a British ship that was hit by a torpedo from a German U-Boat in 1942. He survived alone on a liferaft for 133 days, with some rope and a knife, capturing rainwater to drink, and fighting off sharks. Poon Lim was courageous. You giving feedback to someone to help them improve in their work? That's your job.

- *Humility*: I *think* we covered it enough, but it didn't get its own chapter, so here's its own bullet-point instead. (which *humility* itself would be properly proud of.) When you lead, humility is another one of those tight ropes for you to walk: you need to be confident and for your people to see you as such, but if you get cocky it'll turn them off. I think you have a lot of opportunities to display humility, and one of the best is when you're wrong and someone tells you so. Rather than be defensive, you can choose to use it as valuable information rather than try to explain, couch it, or blame someone or something else. *That's* a solid brand of humility, more than acting like you're not good at something you *are* good at. Or being self-deprecating.

- *Happiness:* It's okay to enjoy your work. It's fine to smile, have fun, and be happy. In fact, a great remedy when you are having a tough day is to find a quick "palate cleanser." If it seems like you've spent a lot of time with people in trouble, go find some people who *aren't*. In fact find some students, teachers, and classes **every day** that are doing like they should **so that you don't get jaded and cynical.** When you look at the rosebush, there are roses and there are thorns. Where do you choose to focus?

Get the Newsletter.   Listen to the Podcast.
Join Webinars.

Visit the website for more content!

www.principal-matters.com